How to Listen to and Understand Opera
Part IV

Professor Robert Greenberg

THE TEACHING COMPANY ®

PUBLISHED BY:

THE TEACHING COMPANY
4151 Lafayette Center Drive, Suite 100
Chantilly, Virginia 20151-1232
1-800-TEACH-12
Fax—703-378-3819
www.teach12.com

ISBN 1-56585-803-4

Robert Greenberg, Ph.D.

Chairman, Department of Music History and Literature
San Francisco Conservatory of Music

Robert Greenberg has composed over 40 works for a wide variety of instrumental and vocal ensembles. Recent performances of Greenberg's work have taken place in New York, San Francisco, Los Angeles, Chicago, England, Ireland, Italy, Greece, and The Netherlands, where his "Child's Play" for String Quartet was performed at the Concertgebouw of Amsterdam in 1993.

Dr. Greenberg holds degrees from Princeton University and the University of California at Berkeley, where he received a Ph.D. in music composition in 1984. His principal teachers were Edward Cone, Claudio Spies, Andrew Imbrie, and Olly Wilson. His awards include three Nicola De Lorenzo Prizes in composition, three Meet the Composer grants, and commissions from the Koussevitzky Foundation of the Library of Congress, the Alexander String Quartet, XTET, and the Dancer's Stage Ballet Company.

He is on the faculty of the San Francisco Conservatory of Music, where he is chair of the Department of Music History and Literature and director of curriculum of the Adult Extension Division. He is creator, host, and lecturer for the San Francisco Symphony's "Discovery Series."

He has taught and lectured extensively across North America and Europe, speaking to such corporations and musical institutions as the Van Cliburn Foundation, Arthur Andersen, Bechtel Investments, the Shaklee Corporation, the University of California/Haas School of Business Executive Seminar, the Association of California Symphony Orchestras, the Texas Association of Symphony Orchestras, and the Commonwealth Club of San Francisco.

His work as a teacher and lecturer has been profiled in the Wall Street Journal, Inc. magazine, and the San Francisco Chronicle. He is an artistic co-director and board member of COMPOSERS INC. His music is published by Fallen Leaf Press and CPP/Belwin and is recorded on the Innova label.

Dr. Greenberg lives with his wife, Lori, daughter Rachel, and son Samuel in the Oakland, California hills.

Table of Contents

How to Listen to and Understand Opera
Part IV

How to Listen to and Understand Opera

Scope:

This course is designed as a methodology, a guide to listening and understanding opera. For this reason it does not provide a comprehensive overview of the entire operatic repertory. Armed with the knowledge of opera gained from this course, however, the listener will be able to explore in greater depth the extraordinary and compelling world of opera for himself or herself. The listener will come to appreciate how music has the power to reveal truths beyond the spoken word; how opera is a unique marriage of words and music in which the whole is far greater than its parts. He or she will learn the reasons for opera's enduring popularity.

The history of opera is traced from its beginning in the early 17th century to around 1924, with references to landmark operas, musical, cultural, and social developments, and historical events that influenced opera's growth. We learn how operatic style and form have changed continuously throughout the history of European music, as they were influenced by political, social and cultural developments, and how different national languages and cultures have shaped their own types of opera and operatic style.

The course opens with one of the most powerful moments in opera: the dramatically loaded aria "Nessun dorma" ("No one shall sleep") from Giacomo Puccini's *Turandot*. We are exposed to opera's unique incorporation of soliloquy, dialogue, scenery, action, and continuous music into an incredibly expressive and exciting whole that is far greater than the sum of its parts. This famous aria shows us the power of the composer in creating music that goes beyond the words of the libretto to evoke unspoken thoughts and feelings—that which cannot be said in words alone.

The study continues with a discussion of how music can flesh out a dramatic character and evoke the unconscious state. We are introduced to operatic archetypes such as Figaro and Carmen. We learn that the ancient Greeks revered music as a microcosm of all creation, believing music can change the face of nature and alter souls. The monophonic and, later, polyphonic music of the Middle Ages is examined. We see how the end of the absolute authority of the Roman Church encouraged the rise of secular and instrumental music. We examine the Renaissance, its rediscovery of ancient

Greek and Roman culture and the evolution of the madrigal, ultimately rejected in favor of a more expressive vocal medium: early opera. The renaissance intermezzo is discussed as the precursor of modern opera. The reforms of the Florentine Camerata are examined as they relate to the earliest operas. Part I of the course concludes with an analysis of the first successful attempt to combine words and music into musical drama, Monteverdi's *Orfeo* of 1607.

In Part II we see how recitative, the essence of Monteverdi's style, made music subservient to words and how, because of its forward-driving nature, recitative cannot express personal reflection. We learn how the invention of aria gave opera composers a powerful tool to stop the dramatic action for moments of self-reflection. Gluck's reforms and his *Orfeo ed Euridice* of 1762 are addressed as the starting point for the modern opera repertory. The explosion of operas in the Golden Age/Dark Age of opera is discussed, along with the formulaic reforms of Pietro Metastasio (including his da capo structure for arias) and the vocal abuses that those reforms provoked. We learn how different voice types are assigned different roles. The rise of opera seria and its characteristics are discussed, along with an analysis of the second act of Mozart's *Idomeneo*—opera seria transcendent.

The second part of this study continues with the development of opera buffa, from its origins in the popular folklore of the commedia dell'arte to its eventual replacement of opera seria. The role of Enlightenment progressives in this development is addressed and Mozart's brilliant *The Marriage of Figaro* is discussed as one of the greatest contributions to the opera buffa genre.

Part III opens with a discussion of the bel canto style of opera. We see how the nature of the Italian language and culture gave rise to this type of opera, with its comic, predictable plots, one-dimensional characters, appealing melodies, and florid melodic embellishments. The highly pressurized business of opera in the 18th century is revealed, and we are introduced to Rossini's *The Barber of Seville* of 1816 as the quintessential bel canto opera.

Giuseppe Verdi is the focus of Lectures 19 through 22 of Part III. His career is summarized, and his operatic inheritance is reviewed. We learn how Verdi broke the bel canto mold; how he dominated Italian opera for over half a century by virtue of his lyricism, his emphasis on human emotions and psychological insight, and his use

2   ©1997 The Teaching Company Limited Partnership

of the orchestra and parlante to drive the dramatic action and maintain musical continuity. Verdi's *Otello* is discussed as one of the greatest operas of all time.

Part III of this course concludes with an examination of French opera. We learn how it developed as a distinctly different genre from Italian opera, shaped as it was by the French language, culture and political history. We learn how Jean-Baptiste Lully set the foundation for a French language operatic tradition, and how his greatest contribution was the design of a recitative style suited to the French language. The reforms of Jean-Philippe Rameau are discussed, along with the influence of Enlightenment progressives such as Jean-Jacques Rousseau, who championed a more natural operatic style. Christoph Willibald von Gluck's position as the model for the next generation of French composers is reviewed. Finally, the subject of 19th-century French opera is addressed. Grand opera, opéra comique and lyric opera are examined as distinctive French genres and Act Two of Bizet's dramatically powerful *Carmen* is analyzed.

Part IV opens with an examination of the rise of German opera, with its roots in German folklore. We discover how German singspiel grew from humble origins as a lower class entertainment to high art with Wolfgang Amadeus Mozart's *The Rescue from the Harem* (1782) and *The Magic Flute* of 1791. We learn how 19th-century German opera grew out of the tradition of singspiel and how Carl Maria von Weber's *Der Freischütz* established 19th-century German opera.

The discussion of German opera continues with an examination of Richard Wagner: the man, his personal beliefs, musical theories, and operatic innovations. We see how Wagner went back to the ancient Greek ideal for inspiration and how he conceived the idea of an all-encompassing art work, or music drama, in which the role of the orchestra is that of a purveyor of unspoken truths. We are introduced to Wagner's concept of leitmotif and his revolutionary use of dissonance. Wagner's *Tristan und Isolde* is discussed as the most influential composition of the 19th century, aside from Beethoven's Ninth Symphony.

The subject of late romantic German opera is addressed and exemplified by Richard Strauss and his controversial opera *Salome*. We go on to an overview of Russian opera and the concept of nationalism. The late development of Russian opera is outlined from

Mikhail Glinka's *Ruslan and Lyudmila* to Modest Mussorgsky's *Boris Godunov*. We see how the Russian language shaped the syllabic vocal style of Russian opera and how Russian rhythms, with their asymmetrical groupings of accents, are distinct from Italian, German and French rhythms.

The course draws to its conclusion with an overview of opera verismo, a 19th/20th century genre that favors depictions of the darker side of the human condition. The pivotal second act of Giacomo Puccini's *Tosca* is discussed as a transcendent example of opera verismo. Finally, we hear part of a scene from Richard Strauss's *Capriccio* in which the essence of opera is debated. Is it words or is it music? It is neither. It is an indefinable combination of both, with the whole greater than the parts.

Lecture Twenty-Five
German Opera Comes of Age

Scope:

In this study we learn how German opera owed its evolution to German folklore and the specific requirements of the German language. We see how it came into being with Mozart's *The Magic Flute* of 1791, and how it was indebted to the traditional German entertainment of singspiel. Weber's *Der Freishütz* is examined as the work that established 19th-century German opera.

Outline

I. German-language opera came into being with Mozart's *The Magic Flute*.

    A. The late development of German opera had much to do with both the nature of the German artistic/intellectual class and the nature of the German language arias.

    B. True German opera—in terms of singing style and the type of stories set to music—evolved from native German roots.

II. Language as a definer of style.

    A. The Italian language lends itself to song. It is full of long, round vowels evenly interspersed with clean consonants that perfectly suit the melismatic/coloratura character of traditional Italian opera.

    B. The French language does not have the clean consonants of Italian. Much less suited to coloratura style, French lends itself better to the declamatory style developed by Lully.

    C. German is a language dominated by consonants. The melismatic, vowel-dominated Italian singing style is not suited to German. Rather, German lends itself to syllabic style: one syllable per pitch.

III. Singspiel literally means "sing-play" or "play with singing."

    A. Singspiel as understood today is a partly sung, partly spoken German theatrical genre that had its roots in popular culture.

    B. The equivalent type of genre is England is called a ballad opera or operetta; in France it is opéra comique; in the U.S.A. it is a musical; in Italy there is no equivalent since all opera is sung.

C. Mozart's singspiel, *The Rescue from the Harem* (1782) elevated a popular genre to the level of high art at a single stroke.

IV. *The Magic Flute* (1791) was the last major work Mozart completed before his death. It was commissioned by librettist/director/actor Emanuel Schikeneder for performance at a *burgtheater*, a type of music hall, offering lower-middle-class entertainment. Mozart was working within a German tradition, but the tradition becomes operatic in his hands.

A. *The Magic Flute* is half fairy-tale, filled with strange exotic people, beings, events and locales, and half morality play about Masonic initiation ritual and Enlightenment ideals.

B. Its music is brilliant and popular, with folk-like directness and memorableness. Musical example: "Der Vogelfänger bin ich ja"

V. A German operatic tradition is born.

A. German opera grew out of the popular tradition of singspiel.
1. Melodies are well suited to the characteristics of the German language, and spoken dialogue replaces dry recitative. Arias are simple in form; melodies are repeated and non-melismatic.
2. Plots and story lines draw on German folktales with their supernatural characters and situations.

B. Lacking a long, commercially profitable tradition, 19th-century German opera became an experimental genre.

VI. Carl Maria von Weber's *Der Freischütz* (1821) is the definitive work that established 19th-century German opera.

A. The characteristics of 19th-century German opera are exemplified by *Der Freischütz*.
1. Plots are drawn from medieval history, legend or fairy-tale.
2. Stories typically include supernatural beings and happenings.
3. They stress wild, mysterious, and uncontrolled nature.
4. Supernatural incidents are essential plot elements.
5. Human characters often become the agents of supernatural forces.

6. The triumph of good over evil is often interpreted in terms of salvation or redemption.

B. *Der Freischütz* is one of the most influential operas of the nineteenth century. The famous Wolf's Glen Scene is a brilliant depiction of supernatural horror, completely different from contemporary Italian bel canto opera and French grand and lyric opera in terms of the pervasive use of spoken dialogue, expressive content, and compositional technique. The content of background music is very strong and essential to the drama. Musical example: excerpts from the Wolf's Glen Scene.

Lecture Twenty-Five—Transcript
German Opera Comes of Age

Welcome to "How to Listen to and Understand Opera." This is Lecture 25, a lecture entitled "German Opera Comes of Age."

First, my friends, early German opera, a very quick history. German language opera, as an internationally-recognized genre of opera distinct then from the Italian and French operas we have studied, came into being in 1791 with the creation and production of Mozart's *The Magic Flute*. By comparison, Italian opera came into being in 1600 with Peri's *Euridice*, perhaps even earlier with Peri's *Daphne*. There's been at least 191 years from the creation of the first internationally-recognized Italian opera to the first such German opera. A distinctly French opera came into being in 1669, at least a French operatic institution, The Royal Academy of Paris; that's 122 years before *The Magic Flute*. The Germans really seem to be carrying up the tail end on this one, so we must ask ourselves the question, why so late? Why did it take so long for a distinctly German operatic school to evolve? As usual, the answer has to do with national spirit and language.

First, national spirit. Despite the fact that Italian opera was a popular form of entertainment at German courts, the overblown and improbable nature of these operas simply did not resonate with the more serious and logical nature of the German artistic, intellectual community. Indeed, this sounds like I'm stereotyping and I am; but it's necessary that we do this. Let me extend this question and get provincial for a moment. Let's pretend that this is post-Revolutionary United States, 1785. What sort of operas would composers in America be composing if they were composing operas in 1785? Would the overblown characters of Italian opera seria or the silly, yet wonderful plots of Italian opera buffa appeal to the young nation of the United States? Would there be a community to watch these operas, to create these operas, to perform these operas? No, I would say not. At that time, America was nation-building. It was a young, energized, mercantile nation beginning to push at its frontiers. The overblown character of Italian opera seria, the silly and entertaining character of opera buffa, had nothing in common with the spirit of America in 1785. While some people in 1785 in Philadelphia or New York might have chosen to consume Italian opera as entertainment, the huge edifice and structures you need to create, perform, and sustain opera as a tradition would not have existed then, at least not have existed for the arcanity of Italian opera seria and buffa. So, national spirit does have a lot to do with the kind of operas someone writes in a country.

Now I said the other reason why German language opera evolved late had to do with language. This is a very important point, and I'm going to spend a couple of minutes here. Seventeenth- and eighteenth-century Italian opera was dominated by singers—we've talked about that—by singers. Italian operatic singing style by definition requires huge, fat, endless vowels with which we need to develop tone, expression, and virtuoso coloratura. Italian singing is in the vowels. That's where everything takes place, my friends. We need just enough consonants to clearly articulate and separate the vowels. This is singing as it evolved in Italy, and this is opera singing as it evolved in Italy; and Italian opera singing is the standard.

The Italian language with its perfect balance of vowels and consonants could not have been better designed if we had tried a million times over ourselves. Let's just take one Italian word, the word for "Italian," *Italiano*. Let's just play with that word a little bit, shall we? It's got four wonderful vowels: IIII-taaal-i-aaaa-noooo, I-tal-i-aaaa-noooo, IIII-taliano, I-taaaal-iano. We could play with that any way we like. The consonants are clean enough to clearly separate these four vowels from each other, but they don't get in the way. They're not harsh and they're not brutal. We could sustain any one of those vowels or all of those vowels as long as we wanted by a device called *melisma*. *Melisma* is when we attach many different pitches to a single syllable, *I-tal-i-a-a-a-a-a-a-a-no* [professor sings this with various pitches]. That was a *melisma*; not a pretty one, but a *melisma* nevertheless. The point is, opera singing by definition is Italian singing, and Italian singing by definition is *melisma*, is coloratura, is beautiful, long, juicy vowels cleanly and clearly separated by elegant consonants.

Let's compare this briefly to French. How would we say French? Let's say "Fran-çais." This is a whole different story, my friends, Fran-çais. The consonants are not sharp and clear. They kind of blur into the vowels themselves, as does so much of the French language. It is a blurred and wonderfully colored language, but it is not one of sharp and clean articulation. Composers of French opera had to deal with this difference of the French language from the Italian language right away. Fran-çais; it's not a language given to long *melisma*, not like Italian. The vowels are there, but if we go on too long on a vowel in French, we're going to lose the meaning of the word because the consonants aren't clear enough to rescue the vowels, frankly. It's true.

As French aria evolves—we've talked about this, French arias have much less coloratura than Italian arias. Additionally, French recitative is a little more melodic than Italian recitative, because when you're kind of talking in French, you can doctor it up a little more. The reason why French singing style and French opera evolves differently from Italian has to do with the nature of the language. Until French composers—or at least Jean-Baptiste Lully, an Italian-born composer who showed the French how to use their own language properly—until French composers adapted their composing style to the realities of their language, French opera would only be a mimic, a mirror, a poor one at that, of Italian singing style and Italian opera. French opera comes into its own as soon as a proper French declamatory style is achieved; and that's achieved by Lully.

Back to where we are today, apropos of German opera. Say what you like about the French language, but it's still a Romance language; that is, a Roman-based language, and it shares much in common with Italian. III-taaal-i-aaa-nooo. Fraaan-çaaais. Deutsch!—that, my friends, is a whole new ball game. Deutsch! Where or where do we put *melisma* in German? I don't know, Deuuutsch? No, this is a language dominated by consonants, dominated by articulation, dominated by attack, a spiky language of understated vowels and overwhelming consonants. It is not a language given to *melisma*.

How are we going to do traditional Italian singing style filled with coloratura, filled with *melisma*, in the German language? We're not. We could try to force that Italian singing style onto the German language, and that's what was done during the 1600s and 1700s; but that's not German opera, that's just Italian opera being sung poorly in German. We've all had the experience—by the way, I trust we've all had the experience, because we should have it once—of hearing an Italian opera sung in English, and it sounds stupid. Aside from the fact that we actually understand the words and it comes of a shock sometimes to hear how dumb these words really are, we also hear a language not suited to the *melisma* that was properly written for a very different sort of language. English is a Germanic language, and of course German, filled with consonants and short vowels, cannot be used in an Italian style.

I mention all of this because true German opera, in terms of both singing style and the nature of its plots, will have to evolve from native German roots and not by imitating and adapting Italian opera as the French essentially did in creating a French national opera. German singing style demands what we call a syllabic setting; that is, one pitch per syllable, one syllable per pitch, as opposed to the melismatic settings of Italian opera.

Do you remember, by the way, when we talked about the "War of the Buffoons" and Rousseau made that statement that the French language was not suited to opera singing? This is all he was talking about. Of course, it wasn't really true; the French language can be adapted to opera singing. What he was saying is that the French language is not Italian, and that's true. No language is Italian, but, my friends, if the French language is not Italian, then the German language is Martian. Again, until a specific kind of singing style based on the nature of the German language can evolve, one that is syllabic in its setting, we're not going to have a true German operatic tradition. German opera will not evolve from Italian opera or from French opera. German opera is going to have to evolve from native German roots that already accept the nature of the German language.

This brings us to *singspiel*, literally "sing-play," or "a play with singing." This is a German play with music. Singspiel is a very general word. In the seventeenth century, this word was applied to virtually any stage work that included music, vocal music—from song and dance troupes to Italian opera. Singspiel, as we understand the word properly today, is a partly sung, partly spoken German theatrical genre that had its roots in popular culture. A very important statement; I'm going to say it again. Singspiel, as we understand the word today, is a partly sung, partly spoken German theatrical genre that had its roots in popular German culture.

In England, such a partly sung, partly spoken theatrical work would be called a "ballad opera" or an "operetta." In France, such a work would be part of the tradition of *opéra comique*. In the United States, we would call such a work a "musical," or a "musical show." There is no equivalent in Italian musical theater, as all Italian works, light or heavy, serious or comic, are sung in their entirety. The Italian tradition is a completely sung one; and almost every other national tradition includes some degree of spoken dialogue.

Mozart's singspiel, *The Rescue from the Harem* of 1782, *Die Entführung aus dem Serail*, is a romantic, comic adventure and rescue story. It's one of these singspiels, and it's meant to be a popular entertainment. Though the subject had been treated many times by many different composers and librettists, according to historian Claude Palisca, "Mozart in one stroke raised the German singspiel into the realm of great art without altering any of its established features." In 1782, with his piece *The Rescue from the Harem*, Mozart takes a popular and common entertainment and elevates it because of his extraordinary talent; and it is Mozart's use of singspiel that will put German opera on the map. Again, a genre that evolves from common German roots, heightened and elevated by a great composer, becomes an internationally recognized operatic form.

Of course, it is *The Magic Flute*, which is also a singspiel, of 1791 that puts German opera on the international map. It's the last major work that Mozart completed. Its first performance was September 30th of 1791; Mozart would be dead in less than three months. It was commissioned by librettist/director/actor, Emanuel Schikeneder, who also wrote the libretto—or a good portion of the libretto. Schikeneder took credit for writing the libretto of *The Magic Flute*, but history has proven him a bit conceited in this one. Others had a hand in it; indeed Mozart probably also had a major hand in preparing this libretto. But we give Schikeneder credit as librettist, nevertheless. He was also the first Papageno, in the opening production.

This piece was commissioned for performance, *The Magic Flute* was, at a *burgtheater*—that is, at a music hall, as opposed to the *Hofstheater*, the Imperial Opera House where *The Marriage of Figaro* was produced. The *burgtheater* meant that this was meant, *The Magic Flute*, for middle- and lower-middle-class entertainment, as popular entertainment. Again, Mozart through his incredible talent and art elevates a popular form to a level theretofore unimagined. He's working within the German tradition, but the tradition becomes operatic in its substance, due to his talent.

The plot of *The Magic Flute*—which is that first internationally recognized German opera, and that's why we start German opera with *The Magic Flute*—the plot is half fairy-tale and half morality play. First, the fairy-tale part: *The Magic Flute* is filled with strange, exotic and supernatural people, beings and animals. The action takes place in an ancient, Egyptian fantasy world. My kids loved and still love *The Magic Flute* because of the dancing animals and the strange scenes and the weird costumes and wonderful creatures. It's got an exotic fairy-tale element to it; but it also is a subtle and profound morality play. It's about Masonic initiation ritual and Enlightenment ideals. Schikeneder and Mozart were Masonic brothers and they both believed, as so many Enlightenment people did, in the message of brotherhood and Masonry. *The Magic Flute* is about Masonic initiation rites, and it's filled with Masonic symbolism and devices. We would need days and days to go through these, so I won't. Let's just talk about the music and we'll listen to one of the numbers.

The music is brilliant. It's Mozart; we could expect nothing else. Much of it is quite popular, in that it is meant for a popular audience. It's popular as befits a *burgtheater* singspiel; for example, the entrance aria for Papageno, the bird catcher. The action up to this point—Tamino, a stranger in this strange land, is being pursued by a huge and, we assume, a hungry serpent. This is how the singspiel begins; some strange, weird concoction, probably people inside a costume that looks like a snake, running after this poor guy dressed as a Japanese in the middle of the Egyptian scene. Strange, wonderful, and bizarre. What does our hero do at this moment? He faints out of fear. Very macho indeed; Tamino's learning to be a man is a lot of what this opera is about. Then, three mysterious ladies appear out of nowhere and together they slay the snake. All sorts of Freudian imagery comes to mind here. We'll keep that out for now as well. Having admired the unconscious Tamino, this wonderful stud, they exit.

Tamino awakens, frankly surprised to be alive. He speaks the following dialogue. Regaining consciousness, he looks around, frightened, "Where am I? Is it a fantasy that I am still alive?" He rises and looks around. "That awful snake dead at my feet?" The sound of panpipes is heard in the distance. (piano example) "What do I hear?" He withdraws and observes. Papageno, dressed in a suit of feathers, hurries by, carrying a large birdcage on his back and a panpipe in his hands. We hear a longish introduction, which allows Papageno time to make his entrance. Prominent is the panpipe motive he plays to attract birds. (piano example) When he reaches the center of the stage, he begins to tell us about himself in a number that has the easy-going gate of popular Viennese music. This melody quickly attained folksong status.

> I am a man of widespread fame,
> and Papageno is my name.
> To tell you all in simple words:
> I make my living catching birds.
> The moment they attract my eye
> I spread my net and in they fly.
> I whistle on my pipe of Pan.
> In short, I am a happy man.

He whistles and then removes the cage from his back.

Second verse, essentially the same as the first.

> Although I am a happy man,
> I also have a future plan.
> I dearly love my feathered friends,
> but that's not where my int'rest ends.
> To tell the truth, I'd like to find
> a pretty girl of my own kind.
> In fact, I'd like to fill my net
> with all the pretty girls I met.

Third verse, same as the first, essentially the same, none the worse.

> Once all the girls were in my net
> I'd keep the fairest for my pet,
> my sweetheart and my bride-to-be,
> to love and cherish tenderly.
> I'd bring her cake and sugar plums,
> and be content to eat the crumbs.
> She'd share my little nest with me—
> a happier pair could never be!

He whistles and turns to leave.

Simple, absolutely straightforward form. It's what we call a "strophic song"—the same music three times, each time to different words; folkish, direct melody of indescribable charm and grace.

More spoken dialogue. Tamino steps out from his hiding spot and says, "Hey there!" Papageno is taken aback, "Who's there?"

Tamino, "Tell me who you are, my jolly friend." Papageno says, "Who I am? Well, silly question! A man, like you."

Let's listen to this, and here's what I want you to be aware of while we listen. I want you to notice the folk-like directness of this tune and its simple phrase structure, *A, A', A"*, the same music three times. I want you to note how it well defines the rustic Papageno. Such music, point three, will have a direct effect on a popular audience. They're going to get it right away. Please note the syllabic setting. Is this an aria or a song? Well, it's Mozart, so we call it an aria; but frankly, there's a syllable for every pitch, a pitch for every syllable. This is pure German-style singing, no *melisma* here. Also, please note the spoken dialogue. There is no *secco* recitative.

(musical example)

Some quick conclusions, please. A distinctly German-language, internationally-recognized opera tradition develops late in the eighteenth century. This operatic tradition grows out of the popular tradition of singspiel. The melodies are well fitted to the characteristics of the German language, and spoken dialogue is heard in place of *secco* recitative. By the way, I have to make a point here. Recitative is not part of the German tradition; however, if we listen to the cantatas and masses of Bach, let's say, written 50 years before *The Magic Flute*, we hear lots of recitative. I want to make a point. Even though Bach is working in German, he's using aspects of the Italian style, and that Italian style will not last in German music into the nineteenth century and even beyond. Rather, nineteenth-century German opera, which becomes so important and so influential and so essential to the modern repertoire, will develop from singspiel. It will not develop from Germanic imitations of Italian operatic style, like Bach's incredible cantatas and masses. Bach's cantatas and masses, for example, represent an evolutionary dead end in terms of the large-scale development of German opera. That's not to say they're not magnificent; they are. They're among the best pieces of music ever written any time, any place, by anybody; but in terms of evolution, they represent themselves, a dead end. It is singspiel, with its spoken dialogue and syllabic settings of the German language, which will become the basis for the international German tradition.

I would also point out that plots and storylines of these singspiels are generally drawn from German folk stories and folk imagery that show a distinct preference for supernatural characters and situations.

Out of this grows nineteenth-century German opera, which becomes an experimental, cutting-edge operatic tradition. The reason there is so much experimentation in nineteenth-century German opera—unlike opera in Italy and France, there is no long-standing operatic tradition and there is no operatic industry, which needs to be fed tremendous amounts of money. Everything operatic in Germany is pretty much new in the early nineteenth century, so romantic trends flourish, experimentation flourishes in the context of German opera in the nineteenth century.

A quick couple of words, because many of you are probably thinking, "He's skipping *Fidelio*; he's skipping Beethoven." Yes, I'm skipping *Fidelio*. *Fidelio* was written in 1805 and was revamped for re-performance in 1814. Why am I skipping Beethoven? Because this is an Italian-style opera written on a French subject. I'm also skipping Italian-language opera. We're not hearing any Purcell, we're not hearing any Benjamin Britten, we're not hearing *Tommy* by The Who. We're not doing any American opera. I would love to do *Porgy and Bess*, but we're not doing American opera either.

My choice of operas during this course—and of course, it's been a very difficult thing to decide—has been guided by the international repertoire. There's been no time for sleepers. There's been no time for obscure though worthy operas by composers like Spontini and Pacini. There's been no time for many, many incredibly important operas. I mean there's no Purcell, no Handel, no Offenbach, Mascagni, Berlioz, Massenet, Donizetti, Gounod, Rimsky-Korsakov, Shostakovich, Berg. I've done no Czech opera by Dvorák, or Janácek. I've done no Hungarian opera; I've done no Spanish opera; I've done almost no twentieth-century opera.

Neither has this course taken into account set design, costuming or specific singers, or for that matter, specific directors like Ponselle and Zeffirelli, and Peter Sellers, who has produced the *Don Giovanni* which takes place in the south of Bronx. He's also produced a *Cosi fan tutte* which takes place in a diner. The reason why I haven't talked about these aspects of set design and costuming and singers and directors is because they are production-dependent. If we don't see that specific singer in that specific costume in that specific production, then what I'm giving you is essentially meaningless. Words and music have been my guide, and the concept of composer and dramatist has been my mantra. Let's continue with the understanding that I'm leaving out more than I'm including. So be it.

The character of nineteenth-century German opera. The definitive work that established German romantic opera was Weber's *Der Freischütz*, literally *The Free Shooter*, but we generally call this opera *The Magic Bullets*, first performed in Berlin in 1821. The characteristics of German romantic opera as exemplified by *Der Freischütz*—six points. As I give you these six points, please compare these characteristics to what we now know about Rossini and Verdi and Italian nineteenth-century opera. German romantic opera, point number one: The plots are drawn from medieval history, legend or fairy-tale. Point two: The stories typically involve supernatural beings and happenings. Point three: The stories lay stress on a background of wild, mysterious, and uncontrolled nature. Point four: Supernatural incidents are not incidental but essential plot elements intertwined with the fate of human characters. Point number five: Human characters often become agents for supernatural forces. Their conflict represents the conflict of good and evil. And, point six: The triumph of good over evil is interpreted in terms of salvation or redemption, a concept with vaguely religious overtones.

Does this sound anything like the people-oriented opera of Italy? No, nothing. Opera in Italy deals with human emotions, human relationships. In the nineteenth-century opera in Germany, a completely different bag of shells, if you'll excuse me.

Carl Maria von Weber, 1786 to 1826. Harold Schonberg tells us:

> To the early romantics the big man, (Beethoven always excluded, my friends,) was Carl Maria von Weber, and a good case can be made for him as the first of the true romantics. Today, very little of Weber remains in the repertoire, except for *Der Freischütz*. Thus, it's hard to realize the overwhelming impact of Weber on the oncoming romantics: on Mendelssohn, on Berlioz, on Liszt, and especially, especially on Wagner. If any single composition can be said to have set off the romantic age of music, it was *Der Freischütz*. In particular, the scene at the Wolf's Glen with it's mysterious enchantment, its evocation of the power of evil, its nature painting and color, its power and imagination, all hit Europe with tremendous force.

We're about to sample two excerpts from this famous Wolf's Glen Scene.

Der Freischütz illustrates perfectly the trends and content of pre-Wagner nineteenth-century German opera. There are four main characters. Samiel is a wild huntsman, the devil in disguise; Max is a young huntsman in love with Agatha, the daughter of the hereditary forester; and Caspar is a friend, who has already sold his soul to Samiel.

Quickly, the story. Samiel has already bought the soul of Caspar. Max, the young huntsman, is in love with Agatha, but to gain her hand he must win a shooting contest. Recently, his aim has gone off and he is panicked; so he approaches his friend Caspar and Caspar says, "I can help you. Samiel can help you, but we must go to the Wolf's Glen in order to make magic bullets." They make the bullets in this horrific scene, but of course, six of the bullets will strike their target; the seventh is made to spin around and kill Agatha. Of course, that doesn't happen; it almost kills Agatha but instead that seventh bullet, during the contest, strikes Caspar, the guy who dragged Max into all of this; and Caspar dies really a horrible, writhing, unhappy, painful death. Max admits what he's done; he's pardoned; and he's allowed to marry Agatha if he behaves himself for one year. There's a happy ending; good triumphs over evil.

The plot is drawn from legend, a fairy-tale. The story involves supernatural beings. Supernatural incidents are not incidental to the plot, but essential to the plot. The human characters are agents of supernatural elements, and indeed, triumph of good over evil marks the conclusion. We could have said all the same things, by the way, about *The Magic Flute*. All right. German opera is about the supernatural, the metaphysical, the allegorical. Italian nineteenth-century opera is about people.

The Wolf's Glen Scene, a model depiction of supernatural horror, the casting place of the bullets. I set the scene; a frightful glen with a waterfall, a pallid full moon. A storm is brewing. In the foreground, a withered tree shattered by lightning seems to glow. In other trees, owls, ravens, and wild birds. Caspar, without a hat or coat, but with a hunting pouch and knife, is laying out a circle of black fieldstones, in the center of which lies a skull. A few steps away, a hacked-off eagle wing, a ladle, and bullet molds.

We hear a chorus of invisible spirits set a terrifying mood, but we move on to the invocation of Samiel. Caspar whispers, "Samiel! Samiel! appear! By the wizard's skull-bone, Samiel! Samiel! appear!" Samiel virtually steps out of a rock. Stage design was something in those days. "*Was rufst du mich*? Why do you call me?"

Caspar throws himself at Samiel's feet, "You know that my days of grace are coming to an end." "Tomorrow!" "Will you extend them once more?" "No!" "I bring you new sacrifices." "Which ones?" "My hunting companion, he approaches, who has never before set foot in your dark kingdom."

"What does he want?" "Magic bullets, in which he puts his hope." "Six strike, seven deceive!" "The seventh is yours! From his own gun it will aim at his bride. It will drive him to despair, both he and his father." "I side with neither party." "Will he be sufficient for you?" "Perhaps." "If you grant me grace for another three years, I will bring you to him as prey." "So be it. By the gates of hell. Tomorrow: he or you!" Samiel disappears amidst thunder. Also, the skull and knife disappear. In their place, a small stove with glowing coals is seen.

Is this scene recitative, aria, or parlante? It's neither. We have three different kinds of vocalization. We have the whispering from Caspar at the beginning. Samiel, the devil, never sings, he only speaks; and then Caspar sings. We have singing, whispering, and speaking; all accompanied by skittish orchestral strings that illustrate well the drama with a very dissonance-filled orchestral background. Please, let's listen to this combination of singing and speaking, that comes as it does out of the singspiel tradition.

(musical example)

Max arrives at the hellhole. He sees terrifying images. His dead mother's ghost urges him to flee. He sees an apparition of a crazed Agatha as she leaps off a cliff, but he's undeterred, frightened, but, "I must have those bullets!" The scene begins with a casting of the bullets. Caspar takes the ingredients from his pouch and throws them into the stove, one by one.

> First, then, the lead. Then this piece of glass from a broken church window, some mercury, three balls that have already hit the mark. The right eye of a lapwing, and the left of a lynx. *Probatum est*! Now to bless the bullets.

Whether this is alchemy or Julia Child, we know something terrible is being mixed up in this pot.

The section that follows is the melodrama. A melodrama is a combination of singing and speaking, usually more speaking than singing, with a constant orchestral accompaniment. Yes, as the bullets are cast, we hear speaking and we hear this terrific background music as each bullet is accompanied by some other vision of terrifying supernatural horror. The melodrama begins.

Caspar, pausing three times, bowing to the Earth:

> Hunter, who watches in the darkness, Samiel! Samiel! Pay attention! Stay with me through this night until the magic is achieved. Anoint for me the herbs and lead. Bless the seven, nine and three, so that the bullets will be fit. Samiel! Samiel! Come to me!

He casts the first bullet, which drops in the pan. "EINS!" An echo repeats, "EINS!" Nightbirds crowd the fire.

"ZWEI!" The echo repeats, "ZWEI!" A black boar passes.

"DREI!" The echo, "DREI!" A storm starts to rage. Of course, Caspar is getting anxious.

"VIER!" The echo, "VIER!" Cracking of whips and the sound of galloping horses is heard. More and more alarmed becomes Caspar.

"FÜNF!" "FÜNF!" Dogs barking and horses neighing are heard: yes, the devil's own hunt. "Woe is me! The wild chase!"

Then the devil's chorus:

> Through hill and dale, through glen and mire, through dew and clouds, storm and night! Through marsh, swamp and chasm, through fire, earth, sea and air, Yo ho! Wow wow! Jo ho! Wow wow! Ho ho ho ho ho!

"SECHS!" "SECHS!" Deepest darkness. The storm lashes with terrific force. "Samiel! Samiel! Samiel! Help!" Samiel appears, Max almost falls and he grabs onto the dead tree. Suddenly, the dead tree turns into Samiel. Max is thrown to the ground. Caspar is thrown to the ground. Samiel repeats, "*Hier bin ich!* Here I am." Oh boy! Goose-bump city.

Let's listen. Melodrama.

(musical example)

My friends, this is completely different from contemporary Italian bel canto opera, in terms of use of the voice, syllabic setting with no recitative, expressive content dealing with supernatural events, and compositional technique. Carl Maria von Weber wrote that "Opera is a work of art, complete within itself, in which all the related parts and contributions are blended together and thus disappear, and somehow in disappearing, form a new world." He's aware of opera as synthesis. Indeed, nineteenth-century German opera will create whole new worlds.

We move on to Richard Wagner. Thank you.

Lectures Twenty-Six and Twenty-Seven
Richard Wagner and *Tristan und Isolde*

Scope:

Lectures 26 and 27 examine the contribution of the paradoxical Richard Wagner to operatic history. Wagner's life and career is summarized. We look at Wagner's theories, his admiration for ancient Greek drama, and his invention of leitmotif. Schopenhauer's philosophy and its influence on Wagner's concept of music drama are also discussed. Finally, we examine Wagner's landmark opera *Tristan und Isolde* as the quintessence of his mature style, and as the most influential composition of the 19th century.

Outline

I. Introduction: the paradox of Richard Wagner (1813–'83).

   A. Wagner was the single most influential and controversial composer of the second half of the 19th century.

   B. Ordinarily we associate his sort of artistic originality and power with the free thinker, someone whose artistic liberalism conveys to other aspects of his life.

   C. Not so with Wagner. He was, overall, a repulsive human being: megalomaniacal, ruthless, hedonistic, arrogant, and racist.

   D. Wagner's anti-Semitism and cries for racial purity approached madness.

   E. Many writers have speculated that Wagner's meanness sprang from an extraordinary insecurity based, in part, on his own unclear paternity.

   F. Wagner demanded from society an unprecedented level of attention and luxury, to the point that one modern critic, Harold Schonberg, states that Wagner actually thought himself a god.

II. Richard Wagner: brief biography.

   A. Early life.
      1. He was born in Leipzig in 1813.
      2. His legal father was Carl Friedrich Wagner, although his biological father may have been Ludwig Geyer, an actor

and painter with whom his mother was having an affair and who was rumored to have been Jewish.

3. Wagner was obsessed with the question of his paternity.
4. Carl Wagner died when Richard was seven months old. Within a year his mother married Ludwig Geyer, who himself died seven years later.
5. At fourteen Richard stopped calling himself Geyer and began using the name Wagner.
6. At fifteen Richard decided to become a composer, despite the fact that he could hardly play an instrument and knew next to nothing about the mechanics of music.

B. Wagner's musical training and operas.
1. Wagner was an extraordinarily late bloomer.
2. His two great musical influences were Beethoven's Ninth Symphony and Weber's *Der Freischütz*.
3. Almost from the beginning, Wagner wanted to write operas.
4. He wrote his own libretti and controlled every aspect of his operas from stage design to direction.
5. He wrote/composed thirteen complete operas. His early works were based on Italian, French and German models.

III. Wagner's theories.

A. Wagner's revolutionary political activism in Germany in 1848 and 1849 drove him into Swiss exile for nearly 10 years.

B. While in Switzerland Wagner took a six-year break from composing during which he reevaluated his career and the nature of the music he wanted to write.
1. He had already concluded that both Italian and French opera were degenerate art forms.
2. He wrote a series of treatises and essays that laid out his beliefs and new aesthetic doctrines.
3. Like the Florentine Camerata, Wagner went back to ancient Greek drama for inspiration. He believed that Greek drama was superior for five reasons.
   a. It represented a successful combination of the arts.
   b. It took its subject matter from myth that illuminates human experience to the depths and in universal terms.

       c. Both the content and the occasion of the performance had religious significance.

       d. It was a religion of the purely human.

       e. The entire community took part.

  4. Wagner was convinced that an artistic revolution was called for, in which all the resources of drama poetry, instrumental music, song, acting, gesture, costume, and scenery would be combined in the theatrical presentation of myth.

  5. Wagner called his projected, all-encompassing music dramas *Gesamtkunstwerk*, the all-inclusive art form.

  6. A key to the concept of *Gesamtkunstwerk* was the orchestra, which had to perform for Wagner the same function as the chorus in a Greek drama. To achieve this orchestral/instrumental independence, Wagner invented the concept of leitmotif.

C. Leitmotif.

  1. A leitmotif is a musical motive associated with a particular person, thing, or dramatic idea. Musical examples: drink/death and desire leitmotifs from *Tristan und Isolde*

  2. Leitmotifs are repeated, altered, fragmented, and developed, often in the voices, but more often in the orchestra. Each permutation offers some new and subtle twist on its meaning; it services to underpin the truth.

  3. In Wagner's music dramas the orchestra is no longer just an accompaniment to the voices. It becomes a full partner with everything onstage.

  4. Wagner would not have formulated many of his theories about music drama if he had not studied Arthur Schopenhauer's book *The World as Will and Representation*.

IV. Arthur Schopenhauer and The World as Will and Representation.

A. Schopenhauer (1788–1860) was a German philosopher who wrote *The World as Will and Representation* in 1818.

B. Wagner discovered Schopenhauer and his book around 1854. It was the most important intellectual event of Wagner's life.

C. Schopenhauer wrote that instrumental music alone was capable of expressing the deepest, most primal human thoughts and emotions.

    1. This was the inspiration for Wagner's development of the concept of leitmotif. A Wagnerian music drama unfolds on two different levels. The singers onstage present the world of human emotions, replete with the half-truths, delusions, and dishonesty that characterize conscious interaction. The orchestra reveals the unspoken truth.

    2. Wagner was also deeply affected by Schopenhauer's view that only through total negation and death could salvation and transcendence be achieved.

V. *Tristan und Isolde* (1859).

  A. This opera exemplifies the quintessence of Wagner's mature style.

  B. Aside from Beethoven's Ninth Symphony, *Tristan und Isolde* is the most influential composition (not just opera) of the 19th century.

  C. *Tristan und Isolde* is a musical expression of Schopenhauer's doctrine that existence is an inherently insatiable web of longings, willings, and strivings from which the only permanent liberation is the cessation of being.

  D. The opera's prelude (overture) predicts the action to come.

    1. It is based on the drink/death and desire leitmotifs. The drink/death leitmotif is composed of an upward motive representing the physical action of raising the goblet of wine and a descending motive symbolic of death. It is performed together with a rising motive that does not resolve, symbolic of unfulfilled desire. The two leitmotifs are mirror images of each other: love/death and death/love, the underlying meaning being that, for Tristan and Isolde, love and death are connected.

    2. The prelude is slow. It has no tonal center. It consists of one deceptive (unresolved) cadence after another, interspersed with long, pregnant pauses. All of this creates tension, and in doing so it prepares us for a story of unfulfilled emotional and sexual passion. The whole opera is, in many ways, one gigantic deceptive cadence after another! Musical example: opening of the prelude

E. *Tristan und Isolde* is in three acts.
    1. Act 1 centers on the drinking of the love potion. Musical example: Act 1, scene 5
    2. Act 2 centers on the mortal wounding of Tristan.
    3. Act 3 centers the deaths of Tristan and Isolde.
        a. Isolde holds the dying Tristan in her arms and sings her transcendent liebestod (love/death) aria. It represents the moment at which Tristan and Isolde's unconsummated passion transcends to realization at a higher plane.
        b. With the liebestod aria Wagner's music must be, and is, as transcendent as the new reality that Isolde is already seeing as she approaches her death. Musical example: liebestod

VI. Concluding remarks.
    A. Wagner was a paradox representing the best and worst of human attributes.
    B. His music provoked huge controversy and created pro and anti-Wagnerian cults.
    C. He changed music forever.

Lecture Twenty-Six—Transcript
Richard Wagner and *Tristan und Isolde*, I

Welcome to "How to Listen to and Understand Opera." This is Lecture 26, the first of a two-lecture set entitled "Richard Wagner and *Tristan und Isolde*."

Introduction—the great paradox of Richard Wagner. Wagner's dates, 1813 to 1883. What Ludwig van Beethoven was to the first half of the nineteenth century, so Richard Wagner was to the second half of the nineteenth century; the single most influential, controversial, and talked-about composer of his time. Wagner was the darling of the avant-garde, the young idealists, the musical left, the artistic left. His music redefined what was expressively possible in both the opera house and, indeed, even in the symphony hall. Now, my friends, ordinarily we associate this sort of artistic originality and power with the free-thinker, someone whose artistic liberalism translates to the other aspects of their life, someone whose humanity and spirit reflect the high artistic goals for which they strive. Not Wagner. He was, frankly, one of the most repellent human beings who ever lived. This troubles and disappoints us.

According to Harold Schonberg:

> There was something Messianic about the man himself, a degree of megalomania that approached actual lunacy and that raised the concept of artist as hero to an unprecedented degree. He was a short man, about five feet four inches tall, but he radiated power, belief in himself, ruthlessness, and genius. As a human being, he was frightening, amoral, hedonistic, selfish, virulently racist, arrogant, filled with the gospels of the superman and the superiority of the German race. He stands for all that is unpleasant in human character.

Yes, indeed, Wagner's anti-Semitism and screams for racial purity approached madness. For example, in 1850, Wagner wrote and published an article called "Judaism in Music" in which, among other things, Wagner wrote, and I quote:

> Why does the involuntary revulsion exist, which is awakened by the person and character of the Jew? We deceive ourselves if we classify as simply bad manners our natural antipathy towards the Jew. It is our duty to bring to a state of complete intelligibility our ill will towards him. The

hissing, shrill-sounding, buzzing, and grunting mannerisms of Jewish speech fall upon our ears as something strange and disagreeable. Who has not been shocked and held to the spot, partly by horror and partly by a sense of their absurdity at hearing those gurgling, yodeling, and babbling sounds Jews make, which no intentional caricature could depict as horribly as the facts themselves?

In one of Wagner's last written essays, *"Heldentum und Christentum,"* "Heroism and Christianity," Wagner claimed that, and now I quote:

> Though Aryans had sprung from the gods, inferior peoples have deprived the Aryans of their godhead, particularly the Jews, former cannibals, educated to be the business leaders of society. Christ was not a Jew. Christ was an Aryan.

Small wonder Adolf Hitler was to say, "Whoever wants to understand National-Socialistic Germany must know Wagner."

According to Wagner scholar, Barry Millington, and Millington is a sympathetic biographer:

> Wagner, the monumental but frustrated egoist, needed a scapegoat more than most. Large head and exaggerated features contrasting with a short body almost to the point of deformity, uncertain of his paternity, possibly even Jewish he thought; unsuccessful in love, thwarted in career, now uprooted and denied contact with his native public, all of the classic ingredients for an inferiority complex, and one that could take refuge in an absurdly irrational and repulsive racist mentality; but the wound goes deeper still. He casts himself in an exquisitely masochistic identification in the role of Ahasuerus, the wandering Jew, the rootless, suffering artist. He longed to belong. Wagner's personal anti-Semitism is to a large extent a projection of his frustration, guilt and self-hatred.

This is a sympathetic biographer. Harold Schonberg continues:

> No composer ever demanded so much from society; and Wagner was altogether unblushing in his needs. "I am not made like other people. I must have brilliance and beauty and light. The world owes me what I need. I can't live on a

miserable organist's pittance like your master Bach." His egoism matched his madness. No composer and few human beings have had Wagner's sense of mission.

Again, I quote Wagner, "I let myself be guided without fear by my instinct. I am being used as the instrument for something higher than my own being. I am in the hands of the immortal genius that I have served for the span of my life, and that intends me to complete only what I can achieve."

Such was Wagner's ego that it is not stretching a point to suggest that he secretly regarded himself as a god. He was sent to Earth by mysterious forces; he gathered disciples unto himself; he wrote Holy Scriptures in word and in music. He caused a temple—that is, the theater at Bayreuth—to be created in which his works could be celebrated and he himself worshipped. He cast out all who did not agree with his divinity.

Wagner the man remains a troubling paradox, a paradox no one has completely explained. Lots of folks have tried, though, as Norman Lebrecht points out to us, "Wagner is the subject of more biographies than any other historical figure other than Jesus and Napoleon." So, lots have tried to explain Wagner. He remains a fascinating character, both for his own personal psychology and this extraordinary music that he wrote, that is so special and so different and so original and, frankly, so beautiful. I will allow you all to seek out your own Wagner biography. For time's sake, we will touch on only a few episodes in his life.

His early life; Richard Wagner was born in Leipzig on May 22nd of 1813. Richard's legal father was Carl Friedrich Wagner, though it's quite possible that his real father was Ludwig Geyer, an actor and a painter with whom his mother was having an affair. His paternity has never been proven conclusively one way or the other. An interesting angle, by the way, on this paternity issue, is that for a long time it was suggested that Geyer had Jewish blood, and this is something that Wagner himself apparently believed. Wagner was obsessed with this paternity issue. It helped to create the inferiority complex that governed so many of his actions as an adult. Carl Wagner died when Richard was only seven months old, and within a year, his mother had married Ludwig Geyer. Ludwig Geyer himself died seven years later, that's when Richard would have been 7 years old. At the age of 14, Richard stopped calling himself Geyer and began once again calling himself Wagner. At 15, he decided to become a composer, despite the fact that he could hardly play any instrument at all and knew next to nothing about the mechanics of music.

Wagner's musical training and a list of his operas; Wagner might have been a compositional late bloomer, my friends, but when he finally bloomed around the age of 20, it was with phenomenal, really unbelievable speed. Wagner's two great musical influences were Beethoven's *Symphony Number 9* and Carl Maria von Weber's *Der Freischütz*. Because he considered Beethoven's *Ninth* to be the central antecedent of his own dramatically-charged music, Wagner claimed—get this—Wagner claimed to be the only legitimate musical offspring of Beethoven; again, "Maybe Beethoven's my dad." I think he would have liked that better, frankly. Almost from the very beginning, Wagner wanted to write operas; and from the very beginning of his operatic career, he wrote his own libretti. In this Wagner is almost unique, in that he controls every aspect, for better or for worse, of his operas—libretto, music, stage design, scenery design, stage movement, really everything.

Wagner wrote and composed 13 complete operas. We should call them "musical stage works," for reasons that will become clear in a few minutes. I would list these operas; we must know what they are for important reasons, because his first musical dramas, musical stage works, operas, are all based on other models. It's through studying the operas of Italy and France and Germany that Wagner learns what he's all about.

His first opera is *Die Feen, The Failures*—excuse me, *The Fairies*; that was a Freudian slap, was it not? *The Fairies* of 1834; it is a German romantic opera à la Weber, based very much on Weber's ideas as we heard them in *Der Freischütz*. His second opera is *Das Lieberverbot, The Forbidden Love*, of 1835. Again, he's in his early 20s. This is based on Italian lyric, bel canto style. It's in German but it's based on bel canto opera à la Bellini and Donizetti and Rossini. His next opera, and his first big hit, is *Rienzi* of 1840. He's 27 years old. This is an opera based on Parisian grand opera à la Meyerbeer, indeed Hans von Bülow called *Rienzi* "Meyerbeer's best opera." It's a kind of backhanded compliment, frankly.

It's with his fourth opera, *The Flying Dutchman*, that the real Wagnerian corpus begins, because now he has found his own operatic voice; but not before writing a German romantic-style opera, an Italian bel canto-style opera, and a French-style grand opera. *The Flying Dutchman*, 1841; *Tannhäuser*, 1845; *Lohengrin*, 1848; and then Wagner stops, stops on a dime. He takes a six-year break, during which time he reevaluates all his artistic and aesthetic beliefs. When he comes back from that six-year break, the first piece he begins is *Das Rheingold*, 1854, then *Die Walküre* of 1856, *Tristan und Isolde*, 1859. Wagner is now 46 years old. *The Mastersinger of Nürnburg*, 1867; *Siegfried*, 1869; *Götterdämmerung, Twilight of the Gods*, 1874; and lastly, eight years later, *Parsifal*, completed in 1882. I would point out that the four operas that are called *The Ring of the Nibelung*, the great ring cycle, those four operas are *Das Rheingold*, *Die Walküre*, *Siegfried*, and *Götterdämmerung*. They are not written consecutively. There's a long break between *Walküre* and *Siegfried*, a break of 13 years.

Wagner's theories. We really haven't talked about operatic theory, my friends, since we've talked about the Florentine Camerata, but now it's time to do so. Wagner's revolutionary political activism in Germany landed him in deep trouble when the revolutions he supported all failed in the years 1848 and 1849. Wagner hightailed it to Switzerland, where he remained in self-exile for close to ten years. It was while in Switzerland that Wagner took this six-year hiatus from composing as he sought to re-evaluate his career and the nature of the music he wanted to write. Wagner had already come to the conclusion around the year 1840 that French and Italian opera were, and now I quote Wagner, "degenerate art forms," hangovers from the past and not harbingers of the future.

Wagner, while in Switzerland, wrote a series of treatises and essays which laid out his new beliefs and new aesthetic doctrines; and these treatises include the "Art and Revolution" of 1849, the "Artwork of the Future" of 1850, "Judaism in Music" (which I quoted before) of 1850, "Opera and Drama of 1851, and "A Communication to My Friends," also 1851. Like the Florentine Camerata, the creators of opera itself, Wagner went back to ancient Greek drama for his inspiration. I quote Wagner:

> The highest point ever reached in human creative achievement was Greek tragedy. This is for five main reasons, which should be considered together. First; it represented a successful combination of the arts: poetry,

drama, costumes, mime, instrumental music, dance and song.

Wagner is recognizing the synthetic nature of Greek drama.

> And as such, Greek drama had greater scope and expressive power than any of the arts alone. Second, it took its subject matter from myth, which illuminates human experience to the depths and in universal terms. Third, both the content and the occasion of performance had religious significance. Fourth, it was a religion of the purely human. Fifth, the entire community took part.

Wagner scholar Brian Magee comments:

> According to Wagner, the holistic Greek ideal disintegrated with the passage of time. The arts all went their separate ways and developed alone; instrumental music without words, poetry without music, drama without either, and so forth. According to Wagner, the descent from the Greek achievement had reached rock bottom by the nineteenth century. Theatrical performance had degenerated from being a religious occasion in which the entire community took part to being an entertainment for tired businessmen and their wives.

Not far from the truth, if you want to know the truth, but okay.

> According to Wagner, the most frivolous, vulgar, socially exclusive and contentless of all theatrical forms was nineteenth-century opera. Its conventions were grotesque, its plots ridiculous, its stories fatuous. Even so, opera was potentially the greatest of the arts for it alone in the modern world could combine all the arts as Greek tragedy had done.

This is all according to Wagner.

What was needed, of course, was a revolution in opera that would turn it into the comprehensive art form it was capable of becoming, in which all the resources of drama and poetry and instrumental music and acting, song, gesture, costumes, and scenery would once again combine in the theatrical presentation of myth to an audience. The subject matter of such works, though purely human, would be the deepest things in life. Far from being mere entertainment, these pieces would be almost religious enactments.

Shakespeare, whom Wagner called "A genius the like of which was never heard of," had, according to Wagner, developed poetic drama far beyond anything the Greeks had ever conceived. Beethoven, according to Wagner, had developed the expressive powers of music beyond the limits of speech altogether, even the speech of Shakespeare. The artist of the future, according to Wagner—and I will award two points to anyone who can figure out who that artist must be—the artist of the future would combine the achievements of Shakespeare and Beethoven into a single art form, something which, on the analogy of poetic drama, Wagner called "music drama." The term Wagner used for his projected all-embracing, all-encompassing, "outGreek-the-Greeks" art form was *Gesamtkunstwerk*, the all-inclusive artwork. *Gesamtkunstwerk*.

A key to the concept, my friends, of *Gesamtkunstwerk* was the role of the orchestra, how to get the orchestra in a music drama to perform the same function as the chorus in a Greek drama. Wagner concluded that this could only be done if the orchestra played music that was as important and as descriptive of feelings and events as the actual music being sung by the singers upon the stage. To achieve this, to give the orchestra this level of importance equal to the singers, Wagner invented the concept of *leitmotif*.

All right. Let's just take a chance to breathe, because this is very information thick and I'm reducing a tremendous number of treatises and essays and ideas to a very brief context. Wagner is not just a composer; he's a philosopher. He's trying to come up with a whole new mode of communication that grows out of opera but is no longer opera. Wagner hated that word "opera." "Opera," he said, "is an Italian word and what I'm doing has nothing to do with this degraded art form that the Italians call 'opera.'" He called his works "music dramas," and music dramas for Wagner are an illustration of *Gesamtkunstwerk*, the all-inclusive artwork that should be for the nineteenth century what Greek drama was, reportedly, for ancient Greece. The way Wagner decided he could make the orchestra in one of his music dramas as important as the singers was through a device called *leitmotif*.

Let's talk about leitmotif. A leitmotif is a musical theme or motive associated with a particular person, a thing or idea in the story, in the drama. The association is generally established by sounding the leitmotif, usually in the orchestra, at the first appearance or mention of the object that it represents or the feeling it represents or the person it represents, and by its constant repetition at each subsequent appearance or mention of that thing, idea, or person. For example, the key leitmotif in *Tristan und Isolde* is that which represents the drink and all its subsequent ramifications, all the ramifications of the drink—death, ceaseless longing, corporeal negation.

Quickly, an overview of the story so that this makes some sense: Isolde is an Irish princess; Tristan is a knight and nephew of King Mark of Cornwall in England. Brangäne is Isolde's maid. All right; background. In a campaign in Ireland Tristan has devastated Isolde's land and has killed her betrothed, her hubby-to-be, a gent named Morold. Tristan himself is wounded in battle. Not knowing who he is, Isolde nurses the wounded Tantris back to health. He passes himself off, wounded as he is, as Tantris. If Isolde had ever done those jumbles in the paper, the anagrams, she would have figured out pretty darned quick that Tantris is just Tristan with the syllables reversed, but clearly she is unfamiliar with such word games. Maybe she's just not too smart. Anyway, she doesn't figure out who this guy is who is passing himself off as Tantris is, and she nurses him back to health.

Act One of the music drama begins on board ship. Tristan is taking Isolde in defeat back to Cornwall to marry old King Mark. We meet Isolde in her stateroom. Usually, we've got two levels on the stage. The upper level of the set represents the deck of the ship with all the soldiers and sailors and men, and then, below that we've got Isolde's stateroom. Yes, she's in her stateroom and she is screaming with rage. The ship is approaching the English coast and she's determined at this moment to take both herself and Tristan out, and I mean out permanently, my friends. She orders Brangäne to mix a death potion. Isolde and her mom, I should tell you, were sort of Celtic pharmacists and they specialize in these various cures and potions. Brangäne, who raised this little princess from a tiny infant, has no desire to see her die, and so instead, she mixes a love potion.

Tristan is invited down to the stateroom to toast the arrival in Cornwall. What's Tristan thinking? I know he's a big dumb lug, but even this guy's got to be thinking, "I devastated her homeland. I killed Morold. I misrepresented myself, told her I was someone else so that she could bring me back to life, and her having done that to me who destroyed her world, I'm hauling her back to marry the old man in England. I shouldn't take a drink from a woman famous for her potions, should I?" But of course, this is this mythological age of honor and knighthood, and Tristan's honor has already been considerably besmirched by his actions. He has not behaved in an honorable fashion and he knows that. Honor demands that he go down there and drink whatever he's given, even if the quaff must represent ultimately his death.

He's not happy about it, but he goes down and he drinks. She grabs it out of his hand and she drinks, too. He's ready to drop dead; but of course, it's the love potion. The rest of the opera and the ramifications of the potion become clear as we go. Their love remains unconsummated, unrequited. There are more modern terms for this; I won't use them right now. Until the end, they can never mate. At the very end, Isolde expires in an orgasmic haze over the recently deceased Tristan, and we imagine them mating happily at some higher metaphysical plane, having transcended as they have corporeal reality.

All right. The leitmotif that represents the drink/death—because the drink is supposed to be death—sounds as follows (piano example). Let me play that for you again (piano example). Now let me add to that the harmony that supports it (piano example). Very dissonant harmony supports that motif. This drink should be poison, but it's a love potion—that kills them anyway, so that they can live eternally at a higher level. It's hard to know what's going on, drink/death. There's three distinct connotations in this motif. Let me point them out to you. First, there's the physical act of drinking (piano example). The motif leaps upwards. It lifts, the way you would lift a glass. Then of course, we hear the liquid gurgling down the hatch (piano example). From a purely physical point of view, this motif illustrates a physical motion, up and then down.

Point number two I would make about this, is that down-the-hatch stuff (piano example) is what we call a "descending chromatic," that is, white note to black note to white note to black note. Ordinarily, we associate descending chromatics with death (piano example). Traditionally, descending chromatic lines do represent death, and it represents death here, too. The quaff is supposed to create death, is it not? (piano example) This is not just drink, but it's drink/death. The dissonance we hear in the accompaniment (piano example) represents disruption. The lack of harmonic grounding equals a state of irresolution, of intoxication, of metaphysical suspension. And my friends, there's more, much, much more.

From the very beginning of the opera, this drink/death leitmotif has been heard in conjunction with a chromatically rising leitmotif, the desire leitmotif (piano example). We've heard drink/death connected to this rising idea, have we not? Yes. The meaning of this rising idea connected to the drink/death motif is, likewise, three-fold. The drink will cause, inspire, unleash desire, because this is the desire motif ever climbing upwards (piano example). I mean, where does this climbing end? Well, it won't end for about five hours yet, but the point is, the climb represents desire.

Three-fold meaning: the drink will cause, inspire, unleash desire; climbing, yes, but unfulfilled, harmonically unresolved. Two; only through death, then (professor hums notes), only first through death can transcendent desire and love occur. Third message; falling death, rising love/desire are mirror images. Think about that for a second (piano example). One falls, one rises, both are chromatic. They are what we call "musical mirror images," two sides of the same metaphorical, allegorical coin. Death equals love; love equals death. What Wagner is saying is that only through negation of corporeal reality, through death, can transcendent triumph of the will occur. Now I'm not making this up. Honest to goodness. I couldn't make this up. This is based on the philosophy of Arthur Schopenhauer, about whom and which I'll have more to say in just a moment.

Now this drink/death/desire leitmotif—we should listen to them, shall we? Let's first listen to the drink/death leitmotif. This is just drink/death by itself.

(musical example)

I would point out what Isolde is singing at that moment, *"Ich trink' sie dir,"* "I drink to you." There's not a whole lot of chance that we're going to mistake what this means. I drink to you. It sounds like drink. It is drink. She says it's drink. If Isolde says it's drink, my friends, it's drink.

Let's listen to this motif connected to the upward desire motif.

(musical example)

You'll notice that it doesn't happen quickly, that climbing desire stuff (professor makes noises associated with abdominal crunching).

We feel it going up very slowly. All our abdominal muscles tighten and wait (professor makes noises associated with abdominal crunching) for that little climb. Yes, he makes us wait. He makes us want it, my friends. This drink/death/desire leitmotif will be repeated, altered, fragmented, developed. Often we will hear it in the voice, but most often we will hear it in the orchestra, with each permutation of this leitmotif offering some new and subtle twist on its meaning.

There are lots of other leitmotifs in *Tristan und Isolde,* aside from drink, death and desire. Obviously, even the most prepared listener cannot decode all the leitmotifs as they fly by, and Wagner does not expect us to. He does want us to be aware of this second, often unconscious level of experience, of truth, of drama that the orchestral leitmotifs provide in tandem with the singers themselves. He wants us to at least be aware that they're there and that they're providing an underpinning of truth that is as important as anything the singers sing. Therefore, the orchestra in a Wagner music drama is no longer just an accompaniment or support to the voices, but rather it is a full partner with everything that's happening on the stage. Via leitmotifs, truths can be told by the orchestra, feelings can be described, conscious and unconscious states can be evoked that go beyond and sometimes even stand in direct contradiction to what's occurring onstage. The orchestra becomes like the subtitles and music track at a foreign film, a purveyor of truth in an otherwise murky dramatic sea.

The composition of *Tristan und Isolde,* and many of Wagner's extraordinary compositional innovations, would have been impossible without Wagner's exposure to, really his complete infatuation with, Arthur Schopenhauer's book *The World as Will and Representation.* Bear with me a little longer. We'll get to the music soon enough. We're almost done with our prelims, but we've got to deal with Arthur Schopenhauer and *The World as Will and Representation.*

Arthur Schopenhauer was a German philosopher who lived from 1788 to 1860. He was 25 years, then, Wagner's senior. He wrote *The World as Will and Representation* in the year 1818. The book remained almost completely unread, unsold, and unreviewed until the early 1850s, so it remains almost completely obscure for 35-plus years. Wagner discovered Schopenhauer around 1854. It was the most important intellectual event of Wagner's life. Biographer Ernest Newman writes, "Schopenhauer's intellectual impact on Wagner was the most powerful thing of the kind that his mind had ever known or was ever afterwards to know." Author Thomas Mann wrote, "Wagner's acquaintance with the philosophy of Schopenhauer was the great event of Wagner's life. It meant to him the deepest consolation, the highest self-confirmation. There is no doubt that it freed his music from bondage and gave it the courage to be itself."

Richard Wagner said in his own autobiography, "For years Schopenhauer's book was never completely out of my mind, and by the following summer"—that's 1855—"I had studied it from cover to cover four times. It had a radical influence on my entire life." Wagner read and reread Schopenhauer's book incessantly. He dreamt about it. He made all his friends read the book and he sent copies of the book to virtually everybody he knew. Wagner biographer, W. H. Hadow, wrote that, and I quote, "Wagner, after the middle 1850s, was probably Schopenhauer's most fervent disciple in all of Germany."

Schopenhauer, for his part, considered Wagner a second-rate poet and a third-rate composer. Poor Wagner, this really hurt like hell; I have to tell you that. Eighteen years after Schopenhauer's death Wagner remarked to his wife, Cosima, "You know, it doesn't say much for Schopenhauer that he did not pay more attention to my music, particularly *The Ring of the Nibelung*." Wagner was hurt, but this particular comment and others like it notwithstanding, Wagner remained a Schopenhauer groupie to the very end of his life.

I will simplify as briefly and as mercilessly as I can—excuse me, another Freudian slip—as mercifully as I can, those ideas of Schopenhauer that most profoundly affected Wagner and led to the creation of *Tristan und Isolde*. Schopenhauer wrote that

> instrumental music is entirely independent of the phenomenal world, that is of the conscious, everyday world; ignores it altogether. It is a copy of the will itself;

meaning the great inner truth—

> that is why the effect of instrumental music is so much more powerful and penetrating than that of the other arts. It expresses the essence behind appearance. Thus, the creator of music reveals the inner truth of the world.

This belief, that only instrumental music is capable of telling the ultimate truths, of touching the will, helped Wagner shape this new concept of leitmotif and the orchestra. For Wagner the orchestra became the truth, the will. A Wagnerian music drama unfolds, then, at two completely different levels. The singers onstage present the phenomenal world of the everyday, replete with the half-truths, the delusions, the unrealities and dishonesty that characterize our appearance, that is, our conscious interactions. The orchestra, speaking without the intervention of words, tells the truth.

Wagner was also deeply affected by Schopenhauer's almost Buddhist view that only through total personal negation and death could salvation and transcendence, transfiguration, what they would call *"Verklärung,"* be achieved. Wagner was no more willing to renounce and abandon earthly life and pleasure than was Schopenhauer, but he found the idea of negation profoundly inspiring and ennobling. All right, Wagner was a hypocrite. I would ask who of us is not. It was the least of Wagner's sins.

Tristan und Isolde, 1859; it is the quintessence of Wagner's mature style. Along with Beethoven's *Ninth Symphony*, it is the single most influential composition of the nineteenth century; not just the single most influential opera, my friends, the single most influential composition, along with Beethoven's *Ninth*, of the nineteenth century. Its influence is felt well into the twentieth century. *Tristan und Isolde* is a sort of musical equivalent of Schopenhauer's doctrine that existence is an inherently insatiable web of longings, willings, and strivings from which the only permanent liberation is the cessation of being. In *Tristan und Isolde*, both Tristan and Isolde ultimately embrace death, not only as the cessation of their otherwise unfulfillable longing, but also as the loss of self-identity in an ultimate merging with one another. Of course, on the basis of Schopenhauer's philosophy they will be united not just with themselves but with everything and everybody else that has died as well, that includes buses and plants and rabbis. Wagner's not going to like that part of Schopenhauer's philosophy.

As Robert Donington points out, "Whatever Buddhist annihilation may mean, it does not mean that the journey ends with lovers meeting." He's right. It doesn't. Oh well! Like Sportin' Life in Gershwin's *Porgy and Bess*, who sings, "I take the gospel whenever it's possible, but with a grain of salt," might I suggest that Wagner will take the gospel of Schopenhauer only up to the point at which it's useful; and that, my friends, is as it should be.

Tristan und Isolde begins with an introduction, an overture, a prelude. This is an opera about unfulfilled emotional and sexual passion. How does this overture prepare us for such a story? Let us listen, talk about it briefly, take our lecture break; and talk about it some more. How does this overture prepare us for a story about unfulfilled emotional passion?

(musical example)

How does this overture prepare us for a story about unfulfilled emotional and sexual passion? It does it real well, because it in itself feels unfulfilled. We don't have a tonal center. We don't have a beat. Instead, we have these slithering and sliding cadences; nothing satisfactorily resolves, and nothing will, until the last chord of the opera as Isolde expires, in about five hours. Is this any way to begin a five-hour opera? Well, you bet it is! Wagner creates tension as we wait for the music to resolve, to get somewhere—and it never really does. This is, of course, symbolic of Tristan and Isolde's earthly relationship, unconsummated, unrequited, profoundly unsatisfying.

Not everyone liked waiting so long for something to happen. Eduard Hanslick, the famed music critic and contemporary of Wagner's, wrote, "The prelude to *Tristan und Isolde* reminds me of the old Italian paintings of a martyr whose intestines are slowly unwound from the body on a reel." Rossini wrote, "Mr. Wagner's music has beautiful moments but bad quarters of an hour." Yes, indeed, we must be patient with Wagner's time demands. His particular artistic megalomania demands not just our attention, but great chunks of our time.

On that note, let us take our lecture break. When we return, *Tristan and Isolde*. We'll talk about the three acts as based on three actions. Thank you.

Lecture Twenty-Seven—Transcript
Richard Wagner and *Tristan und Isolde*, II

Welcome back to "How to Listen to and Understand Opera." This is Lecture 27, the second of a two-lecture set entitled "Richard Wagner and *Tristan und Isolde*." We pick back up with a couple of overview statements, and then we move directly to the music. *Tristan und Isolde* is an opera in three acts, based on three actions. Act One: The essential action is the drinking of the love potion. Act Two: The essential action is the mortal wounding of Tristan. In Act Three, the death of both Tristan and Isolde.

Let us go back to the moment during which the drink is draught, Act One, the famous philter or horned-cup scene, the drinking of the love/death, whatever, potion. All right, an essential leitmotif review, just as a reminder because we're going to hear lots of these in just a minute. First, the drink/death motive—representing as it does the physical action of drinking, the action of liquid going down; but of course, also the death that Isolde believes this drink will bring about (piano example). The dissonance inherent in the harmony representing the dissonance that this will cause, the lack of stability, the lack of anchoring that will result from this harmonic dissonance.

Then we had a new motive added to this one, the desire motif. I keep saying "motive" and "motif;" they're the same thing. I grew up in a part of the country where to say "motif" would have one branded as a hopeless "snot," and you'd probably have all parts of your body twisted and bent as a result; so it would be better to say "motive" from where I'm from. Of course, Wagner calls them "leitmotifs," so I would use "motif" apropos of Wagner. You'll excuse me for slipping in and out of my native tongue, as it were. In any case, the desire motif is attached to the, if you'll excuse me, butt end of our drink/death motif this way: (piano example) and now desire: (piano example).

Let's hear that drink/death/desire motif (musical example).

Please, let's go back to the overture. The first thing we hear when we sit down and listen to this orchestral prelude is the drink/death/desire motif three times, each time a little higher than the last, so we're always being ratcheted up higher, higher, higher, but with a total lack of resolution.

Then we hear a portion of the desire motif played this way (piano example); all this rising stuff and all these silences in between the rising stuff, creating ever more yearning for resolution. Finally, it seems the music is about to resolve. We get this (piano example) and we expect this (piano example); and you know what? We would have had a resolution. That's not going to happen for five hours. This is what Wagner gives us. (piano example) Instead of (piano example) we get (piano example). That is called in musical parlance a "deceptive cadence" or a "false cadence." The music did not resolve to where we expected it to, but to somewhere else.

This whole prelude, this whole opera is in many ways one gigantic deceptive cadence after another, where nothing goes where it should. (piano example) I've used this simile before and I'll use it again; this is like walking around with baloney in your shoes. Every time you take a step, you think your foot is down but then you slide somewhere or another. The harmony keeps lubing us in directions we don't expect to go; and this is one of the essential ways Wagner creates this sense of incompletion, of unrequited harmonic resolution that is the parallel to the unrequited love, which is the essence of the dramatic line of this opera. False cadences; yes, that rising desire motive never rises to a satisfactory resolution. Always to these false resolutions, these false cadences.

I want to play for you again the opening of the overture and now I want you to be aware of these elements: first, the drink/death/desire motif heard three times in succession, each one higher than the last, always ratcheting up the drama one step. Then, more isolated versions of the rising desire motif, until finally we seem to be on the verge of resolution; and then all of this greasy, slick, oily irresolution as represented by the deceptive cadences. It is a brilliantly wrought overture. It predicts absolutely the essential dramatic action that is to come.

(musical example)

Yes, it's an extraordinary and beautiful overture, and it serves the romantic function of the piece magnificently.

Please, let us move on to Act One, Scene Five; the famous philter, or horned-cup, drinking scene. We are now well reminded of our essential motific content, and we are armed to do battle with this scene. Recall now, Tristan has been invited by Isolde for a drink, and he knows in his heart of hearts, in his soul of souls, this could be the last drop that greases this particular tongue for this particular lifetime.

Sailors outside are already yelling, "Haul the line. Drop the anchor." Indeed, they have arrived at Cornwall. Tristan, starting wildly—and by the way, we're going to move through this text very slowly. It's lengthy; this is going to take us a couple of minutes. Two reasons why we must take our time through the text. First of all, it's Wagner's own. He wrote this libretto, as he wrote all his libretti, and he indulges in a kind of "this, thou, thine" mythological language that he almost created by himself for his operatic purposes. I want you to hear, at least in translation, the sound of Wagner's language. Secondly, every word is pregnant with meaning—allegorical meaning, metaphorical meaning, metaphysical meaning—and we've got to deal with the layers of meaning in the text before we can understand the layers of meaning in the music. So bear with me.

The sailors outside, "Haul the line. Drop the anchor." Tristan, starting wildly, "Drop the anchor! Stern to the current! Sail and mast to the wind!"

Why does Wagner tell Tristan, starting wildly, to shout out "Drop the anchor! Stern to the current! Sail and mast to the wind?" He's off with Isolde. The men probably can't hear him right now. In any case, who is he really shouting at? He's shouting at himself. He's referring to the fact that, "Now I must make my stand. Now my honor is more important than anything else. Now I must be brave in the face of what undoubtedly will be my death. Drop my anchor. My stern to the current. My sail and mast to the wind."

He takes the cup from Isolde, "Well know I Ireland's Queen, and her art's magic." He's basically looking her in the eye and saying, I know there's something in here, I've been there before, honey. "The balsam I used that she brought. The goblet I now take so that I might altogether today recover."

Recover from what? What is he taking in this goblet that will have him recover? He wants to recover from his shame, which is, frankly, for him worse than the wounds that she nursed him back from. He wants perhaps also to recover, and now I suggest something we haven't suggested before, he wants to recover from his love for Isolde. Yes, there's all kinds of talk about whether the stuff in the cup is just a placebo, if Tristan and Isolde already adore each other. Whatever. He's looking at this cup as the antidote, a cure for his shame, the cure for his love. What's the cure? Death.

He continues, "And heed also the oath of atonement, which I thankfully made to you. Tristan's honor," "*Tristans Ehre.*" We hear another very important leitmotif and I'm going to point it out now. "*Tristans Ehre.*" (piano example) Yes, "*Tristans Ehre,*" his honor, has been in the toilet since he accepted from Isolde the healing hand. This honor motif will be very, very, very important in Acts Two and Three, when his honor is increasingly called into question. After all, he's fooling around with his uncle's wife, his uncle happens to be the king—not the greatest of people to fool around behind the back of.

In any case, "Tristan's honor, highest truth! Tristan's anguish, brave defiance!" He is anguished about his honor and he feels he must recover it. "Betrayal of the heart! Dream of presentiment, eternal sorrow, unique solace, forgetting's kindly draught, I drink without wavering." He's convinced he's going to die but at least he can forget what has gone before. He sits and he drinks.

Isolde cries out, she is a crying lady up to this point, "Betrayed even in this? The half is mine!" Before he can drink the whole thing down, she wrests the cup from his hand, "Traitor. I drink to you!" "*Ich trink' sie dir!*" (piano example) She swallows what's left and she throws the cup across the floor.

Both, seized with shuddering, gaze at each other with deepest agitation, still with stiff demeanor, as the expression of defiance of death fades into a glow of passion. Of course, for the actors—I'm not calling them singers now because they're acting—for the actors this has to be convincing, and not just silly looking, as they're prepared to die and their features soften, and suddenly passion appears on their faces instead. Trembling grips them. They convulsively clutch their hearts and pass their hands over their brows. Then they seek each with their eyes, sink into confusion and once more turn with renewed longing toward each other.

During all this pantomime, we hear the overture return (professor hums notes), and the desire motive is now attached to the rear end of the drink/death motive; and we realize drink/death have equaled desire. All that material we heard in the overture, including the deceptive cadences, returns as they stare, quivering, at each other.

Was it a placebo as some have suggested? Maybe. They expected to die, and when they didn't, perhaps their true emotions were allowed to come out. One way or the other, the rest of the opera will be very different from that that preceded the drink. I continue.

Isolde, with wavering voice, "Tristan!" Tristan, overwhelmed, "Isolde!" False cadences right and left, everywhere as they can't even sense where they are or perhaps even who they are. Isolde, sinking onto his chest, "Treacherous lover!" Tristan, "Divine woman!" He embraces her with ardor. They remain in silent embrace. (Please remember the stage directions I'm reading you are Wagner's own.)

All the men, outside, "Hail! Hail! King Mark! King Mark, hail!" Yes, life is going on and continuing even as Tristan and Isolde's reality is completely skewed. This is a reminder of that reality.

Brangäne—she's the one who did all this, my friends. She's the maid who mixed the love potion; who, with averted face, full of confusion and horror, turns to see the pair sunk in a love embrace, and hurls herself, wringing her hands, into the foreground. "Woe is me! Woe is me! Inevitable, endless distress, instead of quick death! Misleading truth, deceitful work now blossoms pitifully upwards."

Tristan and Isolde break their embrace. Tristan, bewildered, "What did I dream of Tristan's honor?" It's gone, buster, absolutely gone. Isolde, "What did I dream of Isolde's disgrace?" Everywhere we're hearing these rising desire motives. We know what they're feeling now, nothing but pure desire.

Tristan, "Are you lost to me?" Isolde, "Have you repulsed me?" Tristan, starting to get a sense of what's happened, "False magic's nasty trick!" Isolde says, "Foolish wrath's vain menace!" But they can't maintain this sense of reality. Tristan, "Isolde, Sweetest maiden!" Isolde, "Tristan; most beloved man!" Then a duet, unbelievably exquisite and moving.

They sing together:

> How, heaving, our hearts are uplifted! How all our senses blissfully quiver! Longing, passion, swelling blooms, languishing love, blessed glow! Precipitate in the breast exulting desire! Isolde! Tristan! Tristan! Isolde! Escaped

from the world, you have won me. You, my only thought, highest love's desire!

It's an unbelievably beautiful passage.

The curtains are now drawn completely aside. The entire ship is filled with knights and sailors who joyfully signal the shore from aboard the ship. Nearby is seen a cliff crowned by a castle. Tristan and Isolde remain lost in mutual contemplation, unaware of what is taking place. They are already, my friends, in another world, a separate reality.

Brangäne, to the women, who at her bidding ascend from below, "Quick, quick, the royal robe." Rushing between Tristan and Isolde. "Up, unfortunate pair! Up! See where we are!" She puts the royal cloak on Isolde, who does not notice anything. The men again cheer, "Hail, hail! King Mark! King Mark, hail!"

Kurwenal, Tristan's dude Friday, advances cheerfully, "Hail, Tristan! Fortunate hero! With splendid courtiers there in the skiff Mark approaches. Ah, how the ride delights him, for soon he will be wooing the bride." Ha, ha, ha, ha.

Tristan, looking up, bewildered, "Who comes?" Kurwenal answers, "The King." Tristan inquires, "Which King?" Kurwenal points. Tristan stares, stupefied, at the shore. All the men, waving their hats, "Hail, King Mark!"

Isolde, completely confused, "Mark? What does he want? What is that, Brangäne? What is all the shouting?" We hear the drink motive to remind us again what has brought this on. Brangäne says, "Isolde! Mistress, get hold of yourself." Isolde says, "Where am I? Am I alive? Oh, what drink was it?" Brangäne, despairingly, *"Der liebestrank!"* "The love potion." Isolde stares, frightened, at Tristan. Really, she's horrified. "Tristan!" And Tristan stares back, "Isolde!" Isolde falls, fainting, upon his chest, "Must I live?"

Brangäne to the women, "Help your mistress!" Tristan, realizing what has happened, "O rapture full of cunning! O fraudulently won good fortune!" The men keep cheering in general acclaim, "Hail the King! Hail, Cornwall!" People have climbed over the ship's side, others have extended a bridge and the atmosphere is one of expectation of the arrival of those who have been awaited, as the curtain falls on Act One.

Wow! Wow! We've got to listen to this scene now. It's an amazing scene of metamorphosis from pre-drink Tristan and Isolde, through the music of the overture once again, which, of course, they pantomime to; and then this extraordinary change of heart, of character, of reality, that represents, frankly, the rest of the opera. Please note the following—continuous music. Obviously there are no breaks. There is no differentiation between recitative and aria, arioso and recitative; all is through-composed. The orchestra is equal in importance to the voices. Note the incredible dramatic thrust utterly true to the text and, of course, this amazing, truly exquisitely amazing music; music grown from native German roots, not from Italian or French operatic tradition.

All right. Let's listen. (musical example)

It's an extraordinary finale, if we could call it that. I cannot encourage you more than to say please use your libretto when you can, not when you're driving. To look at the words and follow the music while you're looking at the words makes such a difference, the comprehensibility, the understanding of the actions. Our imaginations come alive and we see the performance; we imagine the stage set. We're aware of movement if we can follow the words while we hear the music. Certainly, in a Wagnerian music drama like this there is so much happening all at once, there's so many important things going on in the orchestra, there's so much activity that without the words everything potentially can get "mushed" together, if you'll excuse my use of a "technical" term there. We would rather that didn't happen because this is music, these are words of infinite interest and we want to do everything we can to get the maximum we can out of them. When possible, follow your libretto.

Act Two, Tristan and Isolde engage in a 30-plus-minute duet in which they sing, seemingly endlessly, of their love and lust for each other. Composer and critic Virgil Thomson claimed that there are moments clearly marked in Wagner's score that indicate—and now I quote Virgil Thomson—"that indicate during the duet that the lovers ejaculate simultaneously seven times." Thank you, Virgil, for sharing that with us. This may or may not be. This same duet inspired the following anecdote told by Ethan Mordden, Toscanini on Wagner's pacing, "At Salzburg, Toscanini was sitting in on a Bruno Walter rehearsal of *Tristan und Isolde* with Marguerite Wallman. During the very long love duet in Act Two, Maestro Toscanini turned to Wallman and said, 'If they were Italians, they would already have seven children. But see, they're Germans. They're still talking it over.'"

Act Two draws to its conclusion with Tristan and Isolde betrayed and Tristan mortally wounded. Act Three, Isolde goes to the dying Tristan. He dies in her arms and she sings her famous love death, the *Liebestod*. Wagner calls this section *"Verklärung"*—the transfiguration, the moment at which Tristan and Isolde's unbridled and unconsummated passion evolves, evolves to be realized at a higher plane. The *Liebestod* constitutes a moment of really transcendent beauty and quietude. It's the climax of the opera, and we will hear it.

At the conclusion of the *Liebestod*, as Isolde transcends her earthly plane, there is for the first time in the opera a truly unambiguous, harmonic resolution, and with it, dramatic completion, as the upwards desire motive finally resolves and comes to rest. Isolde, unconscious of all around her, turning her eyes on Tristan's body, with rising inspiration:

> See him smiling, softly, gently—*mild und leise*—softly, gently, see the eyes that open fondly, O my friends here, don't you see? Ever lighter how he's shining,

Look, Tristan's dead, and whether she's being delusional or seeing something the others cannot is immaterial. She's in a different place.

> borne on high amid the stars? Don't you see? How his heart so bravely swells, full and calm it throbs in his breast! How from lips so joyful-mild sweet the breath that softly stirs— Friends! See! Don't you feel and see? It is only I who hear these gentle, wondrous strains of music, joyous sounding, telling all things, reconciling, sounding from him, piercing through me, rising upwards, echoes fondly round me ringing?

And so forth.

The words, frankly, are unimportant at this point. She's aware that she is transcending, and she is. She is virtually evolving into something else, and at the conclusion, she simply sinks down as if transfigured, dead in Brangäne's arms, upon the body of Tristan. End Act Three; end opera.

Let's listen to this extraordinary love/death, so-called, and then draw our conclusions.

(musical example)

I'm reminded in listening to that of Monteverdi's task when he writes *"Possente spirto"* for Orfeo, this is when Orfeo has to convince Charon to take him across the river to the underworld. It's at that moment that Monteverdi has to imbue Orpheus with the ultimate degree of lyric art, because only Orpheus's lyric art at its very highest can change the heart of a god. Well, so Wagner, here in the *Liebestod*, has to reach the highest level of his lyric art, because the music must be as transcendent as the new reality that Isolde is already seeing as she approaches her death; and of course, he succeeds. He succeeds brilliantly. In a compositional career filled with masterworks, *Tristan und Isolde* is Wagner's magnum opus.

Concluding statements, please: Wagner remains a paradox, a man possessed of the best and worst human attributes. From the mid-nineteenth century to the early twentieth century Wagner's music dramas and his ideas aroused storms of endless controversy. One either was a believer or not. Whole careers were based on whether one was within or without of the Wagnerian cult. The impresario Max Maretzek wrote, "I never discuss politics, religion or Wagner. It always makes for bad blood and originates quarrels." Today, we have a more measured view of Mr. Wagner. Ultimately, he and Verdi arrived at the same place—continuous music, continuous drama—though they got there from completely different directions. Ultimately, whether we like Wagner the man or not is completely immaterial. He left us with an extraordinary musical legacy and changed forever the music, the opera that followed him.

Thank you.

Lecture Twenty-Eight
Late Romantic German Opera—
Richard Strauss and *Salome*

Scope:

In this lecture, Richard Strauss's opera *Salome* is discussed as an example of late romantic German opera. After an overview of Strauss's early life, we examine his psychopathological and erotic *Salome* and the reasons why it is one of the most controversial operas of all time.

Outline

I. Introduction.

   A. In his time Richard Strauss (1864–1949) was hailed as Wagner's successor.

   B. Strauss came to opera relatively late in his compositional career.

      1. His early works were instrumental tone poems—works that function like operas without words.

      2. His three greatest operas are *Salome* (1905), *Elektra* (1909), and *Der Rosenkavalier* (1911).

II. Brief biography of Richard Strauss.

   A. Early life.

      1. He was born in Munich in 1864.

      2. His father, Franz Strauss, was the most famous French horn player in Germany.

         a. Franz Strauss was a musical archconservative and anti-Wagnerian, who gave his son the best and most conservative musical education his money and connections could buy.

         b. Franz saw to it that Richard received training as a pianist, violinist, conductor, and composer.

      3. Richard's classically oriented compositional technique disintegrated with his eventual (and inevitable) exposure to the music of Hector Berlioz, Franz Liszt, and Richard Wagner.

   B. Fame came rapidly to Strauss. For a fascinated and star-hungry public, he inherited the mantle of Liszt and Wagner as a shocking modern composer and performer.

C. The Strauss craze reached its peak in 1905 with the premiere of *Salome*, one of the most controversial operas of all time.

III. *Salome*: adaptation and libretto.

A. Matthew 14:6–11 tells of the execution of John the Baptist by Herod Antipas at the request of Herod's stepdaughter, the princess Salome.

B. Oscar Wilde and *Salome*
1. Wilde was fascinated by the story of Salome.
2. Wilde's play of 1892, *Salome*, is filled with a degree of eroticism, intrigue, and sexuality light years beyond the biblical account.
3. Strauss sliced and diced a German translation of Wilde's play to his own specifications, completing his opera in 1905.

IV. Salome.

A. The opera takes place on a terrace next to the banquet hall in the palace of Herod, circa 30–31 C.E.

B. Salome is a beautiful, sexually aware vixen of sixteen. Her character is depicted in her music. Musical example: Salome's entrance

C. Salome is intrigued by the voice of John the Baptist, who is being held prisoner in a cistern next to the terrace. She has John brought out. His music is almost heroic and lacks the harmonic complexities that fill Salome's music. Musical example: John's entrance, "Wo ist er ..."

D. Salome is both repelled and profoundly attracted to John. Her attempts to ingratiate herself to him are met with scorn.

E. A drunken Herod, dangerously enamored of his stepdaughter, asks Salome to dance for him, and he promises her anything if she does. Musical example: Herod's request and the opening of Salome's dance of the seven veils.

F. Salome's price for the dance is the head of John the Baptist. Terrified, Herold finally agrees to her demand.

G. Salome embraces and kisses the severed head of John the Baptist. In horror Herod orders Salome killed. Musical example: conclusion of the opera from "Sie ist ein Ungeheuer, deine Tochter" ("She is a monster, your daughter")

V. Concluding remarks.

    A. *Salome* is a veritable textbook of psychopathology.

    B. Within two years of its premiere, *Salome* had been performed in over fifty cities.

    C. Though many considered it pornographic, *Salome* is first and foremost an opera representative of the experimental, post-Victorian turn of the century.

Lecture Twenty-Eight—Transcript
Late Romantic German Opera—
Richard Strauss and *Salome*

Welcome to "How to Listen to and Understand Opera." This is Lecture 28, a lecture entitled "Late Romantic German Opera: Richard Strauss and *Salome*." One lecture on the operas of Richard Strauss; that's like having but one sip of a great Margaux, like spending only one day in Paris, or eating, God forbid, but one potato chip. The pain, the pain of it all! We persevere, but with the understanding that one lecture can offer us but the teensiest little taste of this remarkable composer of remarkable operas.

In his time, Richard Strauss was hailed as Wagner's successor. His contemporaries called him "Richard the Second." Unlike Wagner, though, Strauss came to opera composing relatively late in his compositional career. Strauss spent the first part of his career writing a series of extraordinary tone poems, purely orchestral works, which in reality functioned like instrumental operas in that each one of these tone poems tells a specific story and invokes explicit visual imagery. We should think of these tone poems as operas without words. For example, *Don Juan* of 1888 tells the story of Don Juan, but in purely musical terms. *Death and Transfiguration* of 1889, *Macbeth* of 1890, *Also Sprach Zarathustra* of 1894, *Till Eulenspiegel's Merry Pranks* of 1895, *Don Quixote* of 1897, and *A Hero's Life* of 1898.

Strauss's operas: He was a master of the genre from the beginning. This should come as no surprise to us, because for all intents and purposes he had already honed the craft of distinctive, dramatic, descriptive music in his writing of his tone poems. His first operas were *Guntram* of 1894 and *Feuersnot* of 1901. His last opera was *Capriccio* of 1942.

Strauss's three great operas, the operas which made him rich and famous and which have remained in the repertoire since the day they were premiered, were written back to back. They are *Salome* of 1905, *Elektra* of 1909 and *Der Rosenkavalier* of 1911. I would also point out that the librettist for *Elektra* and *Der Rosenkavalier* was the wonderful and extremely good Hugo Hofmannsthal. We will focus on the remarkable and controversial *Salome*, and I leave it to you to investigate the bone-chilling *Elektra* and the glorious, lyric, opera buffa-like *Rosenkavalier*.

All right, a quick biography: He was born in Munich on June 11, 1864. Richard's father was Franz Strauss. Franz Strauss was the most famous French horn player in Germany. He was opinionated; he was outspoken; and what he was most opinionated and outspoken about was his rabid dislike of romantic modernism. Richard Strauss's father, Franz, considered Wagner a dangerous subversive. Franz Strauss adored classicism. Franz Strauss was not just some crazy person standing on a street corner and yelling about these things. As I said, he was the most famous horn player in all of Germany and the principal horn player in the Munich Opera orchestra. This means that he participated in the world premieres of Wagner's *Tristan und Isolde* as well as Wagner's *Die Meistersinger, The Mastersinger, of Nürnburg*. Apparently, Franz Strauss was constantly getting into fights with the conductor, Hans van Bülow, and even, even with Wagner himself. Franz Strauss claimed that Wagner had no idea how to write for the horn. He played his parts so beautifully that Wagner did his best to ignore his nasty comments and belligerent behavior. Yes; "what you say between the gaps of the piece is one thing, but if you play well during the rehearsals and performance, I will probably leave you alone."

Franz Strauss saw to it that his phenomenally talented young son, Richard, got the best music education that his money and his position could buy. Richard was trained as a pianist, as a violinist, as a conductor and as a composer. I would point out, to Franz Strauss's great credit, he did not push his son Richard to be one of these early performers. No concert tours at the age of 10, no exposing him to an adult world before he was prepared to deal with it. The phenomenal talent his son had was, if not kept under wraps, then it was kept quiet. His son received the most extraordinary training you can imagine a musician receiving at this time, and the wonderful experience of hearing live music all the time. Strauss was not just well trained, but he was well maintained as a human being and didn't suffer from many of the problems we see so-called prodigies suffer from as they grow up and find the world more difficult for them to deal with than they thought it would be. In Franz Strauss's opinion, Richard's classically-oriented compositional training fell apart, disintegrated, went "kaput!" as soon as Richard was exposed to the romantic "riff-raff," composers like Berlioz, Liszt, and Wagner. Sooner or later, the young Richard is going to want to meet the people who are hot, the rock-and-rollers, the geeters with the heaters that are doing the big things at this time. Indeed, Franz Strauss was very unhappy. He felt his son had basically thrown away his life and his education.

Once Richard Strauss found his mature voice—and he found it fairly young, based as it was on Berlioz, Liszt and Wagner—maturity and fame came rapidly. Harold Schonberg tells us:

> From 1888 when *Don Juan* had its premiere 'til 1911 when *Der Rosenkavalier* was first staged, the most discussed and controversial man of European music was Richard Strauss. His symphonic poems were considered the last word in shocking modernism and his *Salome* in 1905 and *Elektra* in 1909 caused riots and scandals.

It was to be expected that the conservatives should dislike Strauss's new music. It would be a complete waste of all of our time for me to start reading to you all of the anti-Strauss literature from the various conservative thinkers and philosophers and composers of this age. Obviously, someone like Richard Strauss will be rejected by what we might consider the conservative stream, but even those allied to the progressives had many nasty things to say. For example, Gian Francesco Malipiero in Italy, who should have automatically sided with Strauss's music of the future, curtly dismissed Strauss as "the Meyerbeer of the twentieth century." We now know how scathing and cutting a comment that really is. Gustav Mahler, on the other hand, called *Salome* "a work of genius." Well, Malipiero was wrong and Mahler was right.

The Strauss craze reached its peak between the years 1905 and 1907, with the premiere and popularization of *Salome*, for which he was accused of immorality. 1907, the Metropolitan Opera—after one performance *Salome* had to be removed because of the public outcry it had evoked. The New York press was beside itself with rage over this one performance of *Salome*. Lawrence Gilman, a very influential and important critic at the turn of the century, wrote that he had been bored during its performance. Look, this is a matter of post-traumatic stress syndrome. "Um, um, yeah, I was, I was, I was bored." It has also been pointed out that one of the nastiest things a critic can do is to claim to have been bored. Usually, if a critic writes this, assume the opposite. This kind of tired cynicism with music usually reflects the opposite; that they were scandalized and they won't admit to that; because to admit to being scandalized is in some ways to promote that very thing that scandalized you. So many critics will simply say, "I fell asleep." No, they did not.

Critic Henry Krehbiel was rather more honest. He called *Salome* "a moral stench." A New York paper headline called *Salome* "a loathsome opera." A letter to the editor of the New York paper read in part, "Are we to have our women, our children, sons and daughters, witness this spectacle?" Whenever we want to invoke something, we always mention our children, as if our children are going to the opera house on a school night. Of course, the Baptists went on record against the opera, as did the Archbishop of Vienna. Kaiser Wilhelm II of Germany was unhappy that Strauss, theretofore an upright, moral German, had written *Salome*. The Kaiser wrote, "I really like the fellow but this will do him a lot of damage." "The 'damage'" Strauss remarked years later, "enabled me to build my villa at Garmisch." Strauss made a lot of money out of *Salome* and out of his other works. We leave the last critical comment of *Salome* to Strauss's father, Franz, the arch-conservative and anti-Wagnerian. Shortly before his death, Strauss played Franz part of the nearly completed score, and the old man remarked thusly, "Oh God! What nervous music. It is exactly as if one had one's trousers full of May bugs." Thanks, Dad!

The story, its adaptation and the libretto. The biblical tale of Salome is found in Matthew, and I would quickly read it to you:

> But when Herod's birthday was kept, the daughter of Herodias danced before them and pleased Herod. Whereupon he promised with an oath to give her whatsoever she would ask. And she, being … instructed of her mother, said, 'Give me here John the Baptist's head in a charger.' And the king was sorry. Nevertheless, for the oath's sake, and them which sat with him at meat, he commanded it to be given to her. And he sent, and beheaded John in prison. And his head was brought in a charger and given to the damsel; and she brought it to her mother.

John, or Jokanaan in Hebrew, lived and stirred up his religious revival around the year 30, in Galilee, during the reign of Herod Antipas. John believed he'd been chosen by God to announce the coming of the Messiah. John was arrested and imprisoned by Herod Antipas, partly because of his ceaseless criticism of Herod Antipas's wife, Herodias, whom Herod had illegally married. Herodias's 16-

year-old daughter by her first marriage was the beautiful and sultry Salome.

Oscar Wilde, the author, was fascinated by the story of Salome. His play, also named *Salome*, written in 1892, is filled with a degree of eroticism, intrigue, sexual obsession, and perversion that goes only about a gazillion light-years past the biblical account I just read to you. Wilde's play was hugely controversial, hugely sensational, and was not produced until 1896, by which time Wilde himself was languishing in an English prison because of his overt homosexuality. Using a translation of Wilde's *Salome* prepared by Hedwig Lachmann, Strauss, if you'll excuse me, made like a Vegematic, sliced and diced the play to meet his specifications, and completed the opera in 1905, nine years after the play had first been performed.

Salome is completely within the Wagnerian style. The orchestra is dominant, the music is continuous throughout, there are leitmotifs, the texture is thick and filled with polyphony. The voice parts are mostly *arioso*. Strauss's harmony, which sounded so daring in its time, is no longer novel; but, even more, we can now appreciate the extraordinary degree of expressivity Strauss's harmony brings to this story. Technically, this opera may be regarded as a continuation of Wagner, but frankly, it is more dissonant than Wagner. It's a kind of piece of music which assumes familiarity with Wagner on our—the listeners'—part.

With these ideas in mind, let's proceed. Here's our game plan; and our quick observation of this piece. We're going to meet the main characters, John and Salome. We will listen to the scene during which Herod asks Salome to dance, and then we will go immediately to the end of the opera and the horrific denouement; that is, the revelation of the last pages.

I set the scene: The scene is set on a great terrace next to the banqueting hall in the palace of Herod. Narraboth, captain of the guard, a page of Herodias, and two soldiers are guarding a cistern in which John the Baptist is imprisoned. In a nearby room, Herod is giving a banquet. Narraboth, the captain of the guard, has what will turn out to be a terminal crush on Salome. He anticipates Salome's entrance with the following lines—and he's looking into the banquet hall and he sees her sitting there, and she is, of course, the soul of desire for him.

"The Princess rises! She's leaving the table! She looks very troubled. She's coming this way." The page of Herodias says, "Do not look at her." Narraboth, "Yes, yes, she is coming towards us." The page of Herodias says, "I pray you not to look at her." Narraboth says, "She is like a dove that has strayed."

Salome's entrance; Salome enters, very excited. "I will not stay. I cannot stay. Why does the Tetrarch"—that means Herod—"why does the Tetrarch look at me all the while with his mole's eyes under his shaking eyelids? It is strange that the husband of my mother looks at me like that." Important leitmotifs just fly by at light speed. There is no time for us to define them.

Following this line, a surreal almost Viennese waltz-like orchestral interlude well portrays Salome's mercurial mood swings. We can almost see her going, "Oh la-dee-da, la-dee-do."

> How sweet the air is here. I can breathe here. Within there are Jews from Jerusalem who are tearing each other to pieces over their foolish ceremonies. Silent subtle Egyptians and brutal, coarse Romans with their uncouth jargon. Ah, how I loathe the Romans!

Again, Salome's mood changes; ominous, low instruments accompany Salome's description of the odious guests inside in the banquet.

The page of Herodias says to Narraboth, "Something terrible will happen. Why do you look at her?" Again, a brief waltz-like interlude signals another mood change for Salome. Is she just immature, is she a ditz, or is she dangerously moody? Perhaps a little of all.

"How good to see the moon! She is like a silver flower, cold and chaste. Yes, I am sure she is a virgin, and she has a virgin's beauty." Then the voice of John cuts through, "The Lord hath come. The Son of Man hath come." He speaks from the cistern.

Salome says, "Who is that who cried out?" The second soldier says, "The prophet, Princess." "Ah, the prophet! He of whom the Tetrarch is afraid?" "We know nothing of that, Princess. It was the prophet Jokanaan who cried out."

Narraboth says—he's very unhappy that she's there and he wants to get rid of her at this point, "Is it your pleasure that I bid them bring your litter, Princess? The night is fair over in the garden." He does not want Herod to know that she's been hanging out by Jokanaan. Salome ignores him. "He says terrible things about my mother, does he not?"

Let's listen to Salome's entrance.

(musical example)

Indeed, Salome will not be distracted. She is intrigued by the voice coming from the cistern. She finds out that John is a young man. Narraboth is beside himself, but his feelings for Salome betray him. She convinces Narraboth to bring John out from the cistern.

> You will do this thing for me Narraboth. You know that you will do this thing for me, and tomorrow I will look at you through the muslin veils, Narraboth. I will look at you, and maybe I will smile at you. Look at me, Narraboth; look at me. Ah, you know that you will do this thing I ask of you. You know it well. I know that you will do this thing.

Yes, this is no naïve child, my friends. She is fully aware of her power over men, and she knows how to use it.

The prophet comes out of the cistern. Salome looks at him and steps slowly back. John says, "Where is he whose cup of abominations is now full? Where is he, who in a robe of silver shall one day die in the face of all the people?" He's asking where is Herod Antipas. "Bid him come forth, that he may hear the voice of him who hath cried in the waste places and in the houses of kings."

Please note when we hear John speak we hear magnificent, almost heroic music. John's music is straightforward and lacking in the kind of melodic and harmonic complexity we just heard from Salome. Strauss has made John a man beyond the other men in this opera.

John's entrance.

(musical example)

John proceeds to begin railing against Herodias; that is, Salome's mother. Salome at first asks, "Is he talking about my mother?" Ultimately, she realizes that he is; and he continues to rail against Herodias. Salome is both repulsed and increasingly fascinated by John. She has never seen or heard anything quite like this before.

She says:

It is his eyes above all that are terrible. They are like black caverns where dragons dwell. They are like black lakes troubled by a fantastic moon. Do you think he will speak again? How wasted he is. He's like a thin, ivory statue. I'm sure he is chaste as the moon is. His flesh must be cool like ivory. I would look closer at him.

John, of course, is disgusted with Salome's licentious attention. "Back, daughter of Babylon. Come not near the chosen of the Lord."

But she will not be put off. "Speak again, Jokanaan. Thy voice is like sweet music to my ears." Is she teasing this poor man or is she serious? We're not sure yet. "Speak again. Speak again Jokanaan, and tell me what I must do."

"Daughter of Sodom, come not near me, but cover thy face with a veil and scatter ashes upon thy head and get thee to the desert and seek out the Son of Man."

Who is he, the Son of Man? Is he as beautiful as thou art, Jokanaan? Oh, Jokanaan I am amorous of thy body. Thy body is white like the lilies of the field that the mower hath never mowed. Thy body is white like the snows that lie on the mountains of Judea. There is nothing in the world so white as thy body. Let me touch thy body.

Whoa! She would seem to be serious.

I would point out that I'm not reading chronologically. I'm just reading certain lines. You can read the entire libretto at your leisure.

John responds, "Back, daughter of Babylon! By woman came evil into this world. Speak not to me. I will not listen to thee. I listen but to the voice of the lord, God." John rejects Salome outright, something our young, spoiled, and sexually uninhibited princess is not accustomed to. She gets a bit angry, "Thy body is hideous! It's like the body of a leper." She's repelled and attracted at the same time. "It is of thy hair that I am enamored, Jokanaan. Let me touch thy hair."

"Back, daughter of Sodom! Touch me not! Profane not the temple of the Lord God."

"Well, thy hair is horrible. It's covered with mire and dust. It is thy mouth that I desire, Jokanaan. There is nothing in the world so red as thy mouth. Let me kiss thy mouth."

"Never! Daughter of Babylon, daughter of Sodom, never!"

"I will kiss thy mouth, Jokanaan. I will kiss thy mouth."

Yes indeed, my friends, she will. Salome's teasing has turned to infatuation and her infatuation will soon turn to obsession.

Both these words and the complex music Strauss wrote in setting them caused big problems for the original cast. Strauss himself writes:

> At the very first piano read-through the singers assembled in order to give back their parts to the conductor, all except the Herod, a Czech singer named Burrian, who when asked last of all said, "Well, I already know my part by heart." "Bravo!" I said. At this, the others felt ashamed, and the work of the rehearsal actually started. During the casting rehearsals, the dramatic soprano, Frau Wittich, went on strike. She had been entrusted with the part of the 16-year-old princess with the voice of Isolde, on account of the strenuousness of the part and the thickness of my orchestration. "One just doesn't write like that, Herr Strauss. Either one thing or the other." With much to-ing and much fro-ing she protested angrily like any Saxon burgomaster's wife, "I won't do it! I'm a decent woman, I am." Whether or not she wanted to, she did do it.

Back to the story: Herod, completely enamored of his stepdaughter, Salome, eventually leaves the banquet and follows her out onto the terrace. He has been drinking a lot.

"Dance for me, Salome." "I have no desire to dance, Tetrarch." "Salome, daughter of Herodias, dance for me." "I will not dance, Tetrarch."

"Salome, Salome! Dance for me. I pray thee dance for me. I'm sad tonight; therefore, dance for me Salome. Dance for me. If you dance for me, you may ask of me what you will and I will give it to you." My goodness, a mistake, a big mistake. Herod has not a clue what he just "sayethed."

Salome, rising, "Will you indeed give me whatsoever I shall ask, Tetrarch?" While she says this, a birdlike flute, very seductive, accompanies her lines. "Everything, whatsoever you desire I will give it to you, even to half of my kingdom." "You swear it, Tetrarch?" "I swear it, Salome." "By what will you swear, Tetrarch?" "By my life, by my crown, by my gods…. Even to the half of my kingdom." "I will dance for you." Salome brings perfumes and the seven veils and takes off her sandals.

Voice of John: "Who is this who cometh from Edom, who is this who cometh from Bosra, whose raiment is dyed with purple, who shineth in the beauty of his garments, who walketh mighty in his greatness? Wherefore is thy raiment stained with scarlet?"

Herodias, the wife of Herod, the mother of Salome, responds, "Let us go within. The voice of that man maddens me. I will not have my daughter dance while he is continually crying out. I will not have her dance while you look at her in this fashion. In a word, I will not have her dance."

Herod says, "Do not rise, my wife, my queen. It will avail thee nothing. I will not go within till she hath danced. Dance, Salome, dance for me!" Herodias says, "Do not dance, my daughter!" Salome says, "I am ready, Tetrarch," and Salome dances the dance of the seven veils.

Let's listen to this scene and the very beginning of the dance of the seven veils.

(musical example)

The price for the dance—Herod should have gotten this up front; he might have done without the dance, thank you very much—the price, of course, is the head of John the Baptist. "Aiyeee!" yells Herod. Herod is terrified. To kill a prophet is unspeakable, impossible, but he has sworn, and he's sworn to the object of his desire. Eventually, agonizingly, he gives in to her demand and orders John's execution.

I read from the libretto:

A huge black arm, the arm of the executioner, comes forth from the cistern, bearing on a silver shield the head of Jokanaan. Salome seizes the head.

Ah, thou wouldst not suffer me to kiss thy mouth, Jokanaan. Well, I will kiss it now. I will bite it with my teeth as one bites a ripe fruit. Yes, I will kiss thy mouth, Jokanaan. I said it. Did I not say it? Yes, I said it! Ah, I will kiss it now. But wherefore doest thou not look at me, Jokanaan? Thine eyes that were so terrible, so filled with rage and scorn are shut now. Wherefore are they shut? Open thine eyes. Lift up thine eyelids, Jokanaan. Well thou hast seen thy God, Jokanaan, but me, me, me thou didst never see. If thou had seen me, thou wouldst have loved me. I am thirsty for thy beauty. I am hungry for thy body. Neither wine nor fruits can appease my desire. What shall I do now, Jokanaan? Neither the floods nor the great waters can quench my passion. Oh, where thou didst not look at me, Jokanaan, if thou hadst looked at me thou wouldst have loved me. Well I know thou wouldst have loved me.

My goodness! She goes on and on and on. Her sexual obsession with John has now become something near to madness.

Conclusion. Herod is stunned, horrified, repulsed by what he sees. He says, "*Sie ist ein Ungeheuer, deine Tochter. Ich sage dir, sie ist ein Ungeheuer!*" "She is a monster, your daughter. I tell you, she is a monster!" Herodias says, "I approve of what my daughter has done. And I will stay here now." Herod, "Ah! There speaks the incestuous wife! Come! I will not stay here. Come! I tell thee. Surely some terrible thing will befall." And indeed, the night darkens.

Salome continues to make out with the head:

Ah! I have kissed thy mouth, Jokanaan. Ah! I have kissed thy mouth. There was a bitter taste on thy lips. Was it the taste of blood? No! But perchance it is the taste of love...They say that love hath a bitter taste...But what of that? What of that? I have kissed thy mouth, Jokanaan. I have kissed thy mouth.

This phrase is at first delivered in a monotone. Salome is completely demented. Her lips are covered with John's blood. However, as she evokes the taste of love, the music builds to a shattering, ecstatic, absolutely orgasmic climax, and we'll hear an incredible dissonance at that moment. It is at this moment, with Salome embracing John's head and quivering and shaking with ecstasy, that a moonbeam falls on her and illuminates what she's doing. Herod turns around and sees Salome and sees all that I've just described; and he shouts, "Kill that woman!" The soldiers rush forth and crush beneath their shields Salome, daughter of Herodias, Princess of Judaea.

From "*Sie is ein Ungeheuer*," "She is a monster:"

(musical example)

Thus ends the opera.

Some conclusions, please. Opera historian and psychiatrist Eric Plaut writes:

> *Salome* is a textbook of psychopathology. Narraboth suffers from an atypical impulse control disorder. Herod has phobias in addition to his voyeurism. Herodias is an anti-social personality. Salome starts out as a narcissistic personality, moves to a fetishistic obsession with Jokanaan's body, and ends up a psychotic necrophiliac. Everyone is suffused with perverse sexuality; even Jokanaan is obsessed with it.

The subject fascinated the creative world at the turn of the century. Kraft-Ebing had published his *Psychopathia Sexualis* in 1886, and Freud and Brewer their studies on hysteria in 1893. The revolt against nineteenth-century puritanical attitudes toward sexuality was in full bloom.

Within two years of its premiere in 1905, Salome had been produced in over 50 cities. Some believed the opera nothing but pornography, others found it artistically seditious, and in doing so, they agreed with Plato, Plato, who wrote that "A change to a new type of music is something to beware of as a hazard of all our fortunes. For the modes of music are never disturbed without unsettling the most fundamental political and social conventions." So wrote Plato, who knew well the power of music. First and foremost, *Salome* is an opera of its time, one considered by many the first great opera of the twentieth century. We save our final words for Richard Strauss himself: "One can consider *Salome* a unique experiment with particular material, but not one recommended for imitation." Not that anyone would, or could. Thank you.

Lectures Twenty-Nine and Thirty
Russian Opera

Scope:

This study of Russian opera traces the causes, history, and character of Russian musical nationalism. Glinka and his opera *Ruslan and Lyudmila* are discussed as the foundation of Russian opera leading the way for The Russian Five and the pinnacle of Russian nationalist opera, Mussorgsky's *Boris Godunov*.

Outline

I. The rise of cultivated Russian music had much to do with the rise of nationalism in the 19th century.

   A. The French Revolution of 1789 was a highly exportable model in an increasingly enlightened, middle-class Europe.

   B. In 1848 insurrections broke out across Europe, all of them eventually quelled by the ruling powers.

   C. Art replaced outlawed political activism as a mode of nationalistic self-expression.

   D. An example is the rise of musical nationalism, which characteristically incorporated actual folk music or folk-like music into the concert works and operas of Italian/non-German composers.

II. Russian musical nationalism was a reaction less to the events of 1848 than to Russia's fear of foreign influences.

   A. The development of concert music in Russia was dependent on the tastes of the aristocracy living in St. Petersburg.

   B. Until the 19th century, cultivated music in St. Petersburg consisted of Italian opera, light Viennese and Italian instrumental music, and aristocratic amateur concerts.

   C. Russia "emerged" and became part of the greater European community as a result of Napoleon's defeat in 1812 and the Decembrist Revolt of 1825.

   D. The spirit of individual freedom and nationalism that powered the Decembrist Revolt was felt throughout the intellectual and artistic classes.

E. In and around 1825 certain Russian writers, poets, and musicians tried to cultivate a uniquely Russian artistic tradition. Preeminent among these Russian nationalists was the poet and author Alexander Pushkin (1799–1837).

    1. Pushkin was a Lord Byron-inspired individualistic/nationalistic rabble-rouser.

    2. He elevated the literary perception of the Russian language through the model of his own works.

    3. Among his works that were turned into operas are:

        a. Eugene Onegin (Tchaikovsky).

        b. Queen of Spades (Tchaikovsky).

        c. Boris Godunov (Mussorgsky).

        d. Ruslan and Lyudmila (Glinka).

III. The history of Russian musical nationalism and opera began with Mikhail Glinka (1804–'57).

A. Glinka was born into a wealthy family and received the piano and violin lessons typical for someone of his class. At age 20 he became a civil servant, working in the Ministry of Ways and Communication in St. Petersburg.

B. In 1834, inspired by Pushkin and Gogol, Glinka decided to compose an opera in the Russian language on a Russian subject—*A Life for the Czar.*

C. *Ruslan and Lyudmila* (1842) is generally considered Glinka's masterpiece.

    1. Glinka's score is filled with the sort of folk-inspired melodies, orientalisms, rhythmic irregularities, and orchestral effects that we have since come to associate with Russian music. Musical example: Overture to *Ruslan and Lyudmila*

    2. Story and music

        a. The story is a fairy-tale about Ruslan and Lyudmila, two young aristocrats who are in love, and the sinister forces that separate them.

        b. Near the beginning of the opera, a chorus predicts the dramatic action. This choral music exemplifies the Russian style. Its main features are as follows.

            1. Melodies are clearly folk-like and Slavic-sounding.

    2. Dance rhythms are asymmetrical. The accents are not grouped in twos or threes as they are in Western music. They fall into unequal groupings, with accents falling all over the place. In this chorus we have groupings of five (so-called additive meter, where groupings of two and three beats are played in succession to add up to five).

    3. The chorus sings in unison harmonies.

    4. The word setting is syllabic. Musical example: Act 1, chorus

  c. Among Lyudmila's three suitors is the evil Farlaf, a sort of opera buffa bad guy. Musical example: Farlaf's patter aria (in rondo form)

  d. Ruslan, typical of Russian heroes, is a low voice, in this case a bass/baritone. His grief at finding his beloved Lyudmila in a coma-like sleep is expressed in the aria "O love of my life" (musical example).

D. After his death in 1857 Glinka was canonized and deified as the father of Russian music.

IV. Balakirev and The Five.

  A. Following the death of Glinka, composer and teacher Mili Balakirev (1837–1910) quickly became the czar of Russian music. He gathered around him four young amateur composers (they all had other quite different professions). They came to be known, along with Balakirev, as The Five.

    1. Cesar Cui, an army engineer (1835–1918).

    2. Modest Mussorgsky, an army officer (1839–'81).

    3. Nicolai Rimsky-Korsakov, a naval officer (1844–1908).

    4. Aleksander Borodin, a scientist (1833–'87).

  B. To a great degree The Five were self-taught. Essential to their musical development was the belief that their duty was to create a Russian national music based on the characteristics of Russian folk music and the Russian language.

  C. A characteristically Russian music emerged from The Five.

    1. It utilizes Russian folk melodies or folk-like melodies as the essential thematic material.

2. It is essentially thematic, with minimal development in the German sense.

3. It is expressively powerful, lyric music that is often, to the Western ears, emotionally unrefined.

V. Modest Mussorgsky and *Boris Godunov.*

A. Mussorgsky was the first of The Five to mature compositionally.

B. He was known for only a handful of works, including his masterwork, the opera *Boris Godunov.*

C. Depression and alcohol led to Mussorgsky's early death.

D. The story of *Boris Godunov* takes place between 1598 and 1605 and is based on historical events. There are six different versions of the opera. The most commonly heard version is one prepared by Mussorgsky's friend Rimsky-Korsakov after Mussorgsky's death.

1. *Boris Godunov* consists of a prologue plus four acts.

2. It is actually a series of set pieces, or tableaus.

E. *Boris Godunov* is based on a dramatic chronicle by Pushkin. Mussorgsky himself wrote the libretto, central to which are two issues:

1. The relationship between ruler and ruled.

2. The corrupting influence of power.

F. No composer ever portrayed the peasant class as sympathetically as Mussorgsky does in *Boris Godunov.* Critical to this sympathetic portrayal is Mussorgsky's extraordinary reproduction of Russian speech patterns in music.

G. Musical example: prologue to *Boris Godunov,* scene 2, Boris' ascension to the throne.

H. We are introduced to Varlaam, a drunken priest, whose language and manner is only a step removed from the peasant class. Musical example: Varlaam's song.

I. The death of Boris is as profound and moving as any moment in opera. The old divisions of recitative and aria are virtually nonexistent. Recitative-like music is always accompanied by the orchestra. Musical example: death of Boris, Act 4, scene 2.

J. *Boris Godunov* is to 19th-century Russian opera what *Otello*, *Tristan und Isolde* and *Carmen* are to 19th-century Italian, German and French opera respectively: the pinnacle and a difficult, if not impossible act to follow.

Lecture Twenty-Nine—Transcript
Russian Opera, I

Welcome to "How to Listen to and Understand Opera." This is Lecture 29, the first of a two-lecture set entitled simply "Russian Opera."

A characteristically Russian language operatic style developed even later than did German opera. Indeed, a genuine Russian national school of any sort of musical composition did not appear until the 1830s. The rise of a distinctly Russian music had much to do with nineteenth-century nationalism, so please, my friends, a quick diversion to and discussion of the nature of nineteenth-century musical nationalism and the very special nature of nineteenth-century Russian musical nationalism.

The French Revolution of 1789 became a highly exportable model in an increasingly educated, enlightened, and middle-class Europe. 1848 has come to be known as the year of failed revolutions. That year, insurrections broke out almost spontaneously in Bohemia, specifically in Prague; in Hungary, specifically in Budapest; in Austria, in Vienna; and as well in Italy, Norway, Poland, and, as usual, in Paris. I would remind you that the French Revolution, the first French Revolution, took place between 1789 and '95; but I would also remind you that with the defeat of Napoleon, the Bourbon family, that is Louis XVIII, was instated, or should we say reinstated, to the throne in 1815. We call this the Bourbon Restoration. It would seem, after this 26 years of revolution and Napoleonic era, that we're right back to where we were in 1789, in France in 1815. Instead of Louis XVI, we've got Louis XVIII. Louis XVII died in jail in that interim period. We have a series of other revolutionary insurrections in France, specifically in Paris. We have one in 1830, we have one in 1848, and we have one in 1870. With all due respect and without seeming too "cute," might I suggest that what baseball became in the United States, so revolutions became in France, particularly in Paris. The national pastime, my friends. Get your Red Hots! Get your soufflé! Get your guillotines! Get your programs! You cannot tell the radical faction without your programs.

Back to rather more serious things, thank you. These failed revolutions of 1848, for reasons too complex and too lengthy—I'm not going to get into the reasons why they failed. Suffice it to say that fail they did, one after the other. Artistic nationalism replaced outlawed political activism as a mode by which national identity and fervor could be expressed. In particular, the year of failed revolutions, that is 1848, gave rise to a musical movement known as "nationalism." The characteristic feature of this movement was the incorporation of national folk music or folk-like melodies into concert works, songs, and operas. Tone poems and operas were based on programs and libretti that themselves were based on national themes, legends, and myths.

The result of all this was opera and concert music that stirred strong emotions at home and made a powerful ethnic impression abroad. For example, in Bohemia, that would be the Czech Republic today, a Czech-language national opera developed during the second half of the nineteenth century, to a great degree in direct response to the failed revolution of 1848. For example, we see the operas of Bedřich Smetana: *The Bartered Bride* of 1866, *Dalibor* of 1868, *The Kiss* of 1876. We see Antonin Dvořák's wonderful opera, *Rusalka*.

I'm going to get on my soapbox for just a moment. There are certain composers whom we know from their instrumental music and there are certain composers we know from their operas, but often a composer who wrote both is only known for one or the other. Dvořák is a perfect example of a wonderful opera composer who's known for his chamber music and symphonies, but not so much for the operatic output. I would at this moment just stand here and promote, to any promoter who might be watching, *Rusalka*. It's a wonderful opera and it dates from 1901. Leos Janáček wrote *Jenufa* and *The Cunning Little Vixen* in 1824 [sic 1924]. I would point out that Czech opera is to a great degree the result of the spirit of individuality and national fervor that was created by the Enlightenment and stirred by the French Revolution and the failed revolutions of 1848; music as a mirror, an entire school of national opera that is a response to political and environmental issues.

Russian musical nationalism specifically. Russian musical nationalism is less a reaction to the events of 1848 and more a reaction to Russia's entry into the European world and the desire, always the desire, on the part of Russian artists to ensure the preservation of their unique musical heritage in the face of encroaching Italian and German musical dominance. Yes, my friends, the Russian fear of outsiders would be a constant in Russian history, and Russian musical nationalism is to a great degree the result of Russian musical fear of outside dominance. Xenophobia as a compositional inspiration—only in Russia.

A little background, please. Peter I is the first Russian czar to attempt to lift Russia out of the Middle Ages. Peter lived, in what we would call in Western Europe, during the Baroque era, between 1682 and 1725. Peter builds another Venice, and that's what he wanted it to be, and that's, frankly, what it looks like, at the mouth of the Neve River. It becomes his window on the West, this new Venice, and he stocks this new city with the best foreign artists, musicians, and teachers his money can buy. St. Petersburg, named for his patron saint, becomes the most Westernized and culturally diverse city in all of Russia. One reason for this is that in St. Petersburg it is the aristocratic class, it's the court that holds sway, not the Russian Orthodox Church, a notoriously conservative and medieval organization.

Until the nineteenth century, cultivated music in St. Petersburg—which means basically cultivated music in Russia, as most of the Western European musical culture you would have heard in Russia at that time you would have heard in St. Petersburg—until the nineteenth century, cultivated music at "St. Pete" consisted of the following. Italian opera, seria, buffa and bel canto; two, light Viennese and Italian instrumental music; and three, aristocratic amateur concerts.

Russia truly emerged and became part of the greater European community as the result of two galvanizing historical events; first, the defeat of Napoleon in 1812, and the Decembrist Revolt, which occurred in December of 1825. This was a failed attempt to create a constitutional monarchy based on the ideals of the French Revolution. The spirit of individual freedom and nationalism that powered this Decembrist Revolution was felt throughout the intellectual and artistic classes of Russia. In and around the year 1825, there was a conscious decision made by certain Russian writers, poets, and musicians, a conscious decision to cultivate a uniquely Russian, Russian-language artistic tradition—as opposed to Italian opera seria, buffa and bel canto, as opposed to the light Viennese and Italian instrumental music played by amateurs and professionals alike—to cultivate a uniquely Russian, Russian-language artistic tradition. All of this is occurring around the year 1825.

Pre-eminent among these Russian nationalists was the poet and author Alexander Sergeevich Pushkin, who lived from 1799 to 1837. Though he was born into a noble family, Pushkin was a kind of Lord Byron-inspired, individualistic, nationalistic rabble-rouser, one of "dem hippy-dippy left-wing agitator types," if you'll excuse me. Pushkin did for the Russian language what Goethe did for the German language. Through the model of his own works he provided a literary heritage for a Russian language, which, up to his time, had been considered unfit for fine literature. Among Pushkin's works turned into operas were *Eugene Onegin* and *Queen of Spades*; both of these were turned into operas by Pyotr Tchaikovsky; *Boris Godunov*, turned into an opera by Modest Mussorgsky; and *Ruslan and Lyudmila*, turned into an opera by Mikhail Glinka. Let us move on to Mr. Glinka, the godfather of Russian music.

Mikhail Ivanovich Glinka, 1804 to 1857. The history of a true Russian music and Russian opera begins with Mikhail Glinka. Born into a wealthy land-owning family, Glinka's early musical education consisted of the usual piano and violin lessons. This would be typical for someone of his class, a certain degree of cursory polish given him in Western artistic tradition. In 1824, at the age of 20, Glinka became a civil servant, working in the Ministry of Ways and Communication in St. Petersburg. This should not come as a surprise to us, that someone who is gifted in music gets a job as a civil servant. Educated young Russian men from the upper classes typically entered either the civil service or the military for a career. I would point out that "real" Russian men were not professional musicians. Yes, Italians were musicians; perhaps even Germans were musicians, but not Russians, not professionals. Two points; first of all, it wasn't considered a properly masculine thing to do. There's no macho in being a professional musician. Might I editorialize for a moment? This is an attitude we see also in the United States, really up to the mid-twentieth century. Foreigners are professional musicians. Real men have real jobs, make real money and do real things. Music is for the ladies and the foreigners. That attitude permeates Russian culture as well as it did permeate American culture. Point two; musicians in Russia had no acknowledged social status in the mid-nineteenth century.

In 1862 Anton Rubinstein, the great Russian pianist and founder of the St. Petersburg Conservatory, wrote this and I quote:

Russia has almost no august musicians in the exact sense of this term. This is because our government has not given the same privileges to the art of music that are enjoyed by the other arts, such as painting, sculpture, et cetera. That is, he who practices music is not given the official rank of an artist.

It's a kind of artistic black hole, the world of music in mid- and early-nineteenth century Russia.

We move on to 1834. Inspired by Pushkin and Nikolai Gogol, Glinka decides to compose an opera on a Russian subject, but more importantly, in the Russian language. The result was the opera *A Life for the Czar*. Premiered in the presence of the imperial family on December 9 of 1836, *A Life for the Czar* was a triumph, a gigantic success. Melodically and rhythmically, *A Life for the Czar* owes as much to Italy as it does to Russia, and it employs as well the large choruses and the dance episodes of French opera; but it is written in the Russian language. In it, Glinka devised a flexible and highly melodic style of recitative that well complements the rhythms and the inflections of the Russian language. If we have heard the sound of the Russian language, we know how completely different it is from any of the Western European languages, whether they be Germanic or Romance languages. So a music well accommodated to the rhythm and inflection of Russian will naturally sound different than a music accommodated to the rhythms and inflections of French, Italian or German. Russian national music begins with *A Life for the Czar*, in 1836. We can actually put a date on the beginning of Russian nationalism and a Russian national school.

Pyotr Tchaikovsky, writing many years later, was stunned by Glinka's transformation from musical amateur to, and I say this in quotations, "genius." I quote Tchaikovsky:

> A dilettante who played now on the violin, now on the piano, who composed colorless quadrilles and fantasies on stylish themes, who composed nothing but banalities in the taste of the 1830s, who suddenly in the 34th year of his life produces an opera, which by its genius, breadth, originality and flawless technique stands on a level with the greatest and most profound music. Incredible!

Let us move on to a more important opera in the output of Glinka and that would be the opera *Ruslan and Lyudmila* of 1842. Please, gestation and content. *Ruslan and Lyudmila* is generally considered Glinka's great masterwork. The story is by Pushkin. Glinka had hoped dearly that Pushkin would write the libretto and they had discussed Pushkin's writing of the libretto, though these hopes were dashed when Pushkin got himself killed in a duel in 1837. Instead, Glinka himself wrote the libretto along with someone named Valerian Shirkov. I would tell you that four other librettists participated in adding certain sections of this opera to the larger libretto created by Glinka and Shirkov. This creates a terrific mess. If you want to know the truth, the libretto ain't a pretty thing, and it doesn't make a whole heck of a lot of sense. Be that as it may, it's Glinka's music that's important. Glinka's score is filled with the sort of folk-inspired melodies, orientalisms, rhythmic irregularities, and orchestral effects that we have since come to associate as being Russian in character. My friends, Glinka's music, always like the name brand that becomes a generic designation due to its universal usage—kleenex, jello, xerox and thermos, for example; these are all words that we use as designations even though they were originally name brands—the sound of Glinka's music is what we now call the Russian sound, simply due to its quality and the association of this music with the beginnings of a Russian school.

Ruslan and Lyudmila, the story and the music. *Ruslan and Lyudmila* opens with a brilliant and rollicking overture, and I'm going to play you the first couple minutes of it in just a moment. Here are the questions I want you to ask yourselves while listening. Does this music sound like bel canto Italian opera? (professor hums sample notes.) Does this music sound like upright and magnificent French music? (professor hums sample notes.) Does this music sound like direct and serious German music? Well, does it?

Overture, *Ruslan and Lyudmila*. (musical example)

Well, does this sound like bel canto opera? Does this sound like French opera? Does this sound like the serious German opera? No. No. This music is filled with the wild and, to Western ears, exotic sound of Russian dance, fabulous rhythmicality, great energy, a very different-sounding kind of music. Believe me, start an opera this way and you're going to have to continue the opera this way.

The story in a nutshell; it is a fairy-tale, a folk yarn. The opera opens with a celebration held by the Grand Duke of Kiev, Svyetozar, in honor of his daughter Lyudmila's three suitors. A bard prophesies a wondrous future if Lyudmila chooses Ruslan. Lyudmila herself welcomes her three suitors, and she sings of her reluctance to leave home and the joy that she has known there. Of her three suitors, Ruslan, a knight; Ratmir, an oriental prince; and Farlaf, *sssssssss*, a blustering coward; Ruslan is the favored one. This should not come as a big surprise, given the title and all. Out of nowhere, a terrifying thunderclap is followed by sudden darkness across the stage. When order is restored, it is discovered that Lyudmila has disappeared. Pop and zam! As we find out later, she did not head off to 7-Eleven for a quick Slurpee; rather, she has been abducted by the evil dwarf, Chernomor. Lyudmila's father, Svyetozar, promises her hand in marriage to the one who rescues her; and so the action of the opera is initiated.

What we're going to do with this opera is talk about some of the Glinka Russianisms that so fill the score. We don't have time to go through this opera in detail, and we wouldn't anyway. It's not an opera you'll generally see or hear in performance today, at least not outside of Russia; but it's an opera that's incredibly influential on the next generation of Russian composers. Those composers include such important opera composers as Mussorgsky and Rimsky-Korsakov. Let's observe some of the Russianisms that we hear across this score, so we have an idea of what was so influential and so galvanizing to the Russian community in the nineteenth century.

Immediately before the fateful thunderclap, we hear an ecstatic chorus, which celebrates the wonder and the mystery of love. We're back in Act One. Let me read you this chorus. It's very wordy, but that's all right, we have nowhere else to go right now; then let's talk about the setting because it's very different from anything we've heard up to this point in this course.

Chorus: "O, mysterious, wonderful god of love!" That opening line becomes a refrain that keeps coming back and back and back, of course, across the span of these words.

> You pour ecstasy into our hearts; We glorify your power and strength, which cannot be avoided on earth!
>
> Refrain: O, god of love, god of love!
>
> You transform our sad world into a heaven of happiness and pleasure. In the depths of night, through disasters and fear, you lead us to a bed of luxury. You fill our souls with

passion and you send a smile to our lips. O, god of love, god of love! But miraculous god of love, you are also the god of jealousy, who pours the fever of revenge into us. And on his bed of languor you betray the unarmed criminal to his enemy. Thus you even out sorrow and joy, so that we do not forget the gods.

Refrain: O, god of love!

All that is great, all that is criminal mortals learn from you. You lead us into the terrible battle to protect our land, as if leading us to a wondrous feast. You place a garland of laurels on the brows of the survivors, and you prepare a wake for those who fell in the battle for the fatherland. O, mysterious, wonderful god of love! You pour ecstasy into our hearts!

I would point out what might be obvious and, of course, if you know this opera it's very obvious, this chorus basically predicts all the action that's going to take place in the following opera, talking about jealousy and revenge and battle and so forth; it basically outlines the action to come. It's subtle, but it's there. Then, immediately after the chorus ends, we hear a short but loud thunderclap and the stage darkens. This is the moment when poor Lyudmila is abducted.

The Russianisms that we hear in this selection, in this chorus. Number one; please notice the engaging, clearly Slavic-sounding melody. From a folk point of view, this is not a folk song, but it's a folk-like melody. Glinka is speaking with the inflections of a Russian composer. Secondly, joyful, energized, and asymmetrical dance rhythms. After we've heard this selection, I'm going to talk about what I mean by asymmetrical dance rhythms and the asymmetrical rhythms that are familiar in Russian music. Three, we hear a chant-like opening, a Gregorian chant-like opening, which sees the orchestra and the voices all singing and playing in unison, all the same pitches. It sounds very primal and it sounds purposefully artless. I didn't say "crude," but I said "artless;" that is, it sounds like something that has been composed to sound folk-like, the spontaneous singing of a happy group of people. Fourthly, note the syllabic setting. Russian, like German, is not a language given to long *melismas*. It's a language with very complex consonants, and as a result, a proper Russian setting is syllabic, not filled with curlicues and *melismas* like we would hear in Italian music and even to a lesser degree in French music.

Let us listen, then, to the chorus "O, mysterious wonderful god of love!" When we finish, we must talk about the special nature of Russian articulation and rhythm.

(musical example)

There was our thunderclap and the stage becomes dark. I said we have to talk a little about the different nature of Russian rhythm and Russian folk music, and indeed of Russian language, to understand what makes this music different rhythmically. When we talk about Western European folk music—and now I'm including the folk music of both Romance countries like Spain and Italy and France, and German folk music—we have a folk music that is usually in what we call either duple or triple meter; that is, the beats are grouped by either twos or threes. For example, a perfect example of triple meter is a waltz, where we hear beats grouped by threes (piano example): one-two-three, one-two-three, one-two-three, one-two-three, one, and so forth. Once that meter is established in a waltz, it will continue throughout the piece. Likewise, something in duple meter means that we hear the beats grouped in twos or fours. For example (piano example), one-two-three-four, one-two-three-four, one-two-three-four, one-two-three-four, one. Again, typically in Western folk music and Western concert music, once a duple meter is established it will generally be maintained for the entire breadth of the movement, or at least that particular aria, if this is an opera.

Eastern European and Russian folk music is different. We have a language that's different. We have an asymmetrically accented language in Russian, for example, so we don't have these nice clean one-two-three, one-two-three. We have asymmetrical groupings, one-two-three, one-two, one-two, one, one-two-three, one-two, one-two, one-two-three, with accents falling all over the place. A group of two, a group of three, one, a group of three, a group of two— because this is a music that is well molded to a very special series of articulations. This is how Russian folk music, and I would also point out, Bulgarian and Hungarian folk music, work. We have a music that is a reflection of a language and it's a language that is asymmetrically accented, so we don't have the consistent meters we hear in the West.

In this particular piece we had a grouping of five. This is called "additive meter," where we have unequal groupings, a three plus a two equals a five, one-two-three-four-five, one-two-three-four-five, one-two-three-four-five, one-two-three-four-five, one-two-three, one-two, one-two-three, one-two. If you rewind your tapes and listen to this chorus again, you'll be able to count to five, not four, not three. You will not find groupings of five in Mozart, Handel, Beethoven, in the music of France, in the music of Italy. It's just not done in the eighteenth and the nineteenth century; it's just not done. It's done in Russian music, and that's something that we hear. We might not notice it consciously, but it's something we hear, this rhythmic irregularity, this wonderful, exotic approach to accentuation of differing groups of beats that sounds exotic and different. We have come to label it Russian or at least Slavic; and that's an important aspect of this music, and it's something that would not have been done by a Russian composer before Glinka. Glinka basically says it's fine to do this; it's natural to do this; I'm going to do it. By his model, the whole sound, the whole rhythmic nature of Russian music, changes as Russians accept the patterns implicit to their own spirit, but patterns that they have not used because they'd rather copy Western European models. Point gotten? Point gotten. Let's continue.

Farlaf's rondo. Of the three suitors, Farlaf is clearly the third choice. Frankly my friends, better a monastery than the toad, Farlaf. He's a braggart and a coward posing as a warrior. Farlaf runs with bad company, and this includes a witch named Naina. Naina promises to deliver Lyudmila to Farlaf while Farlaf basically sits at home in his castle in his recliner. Farlaf, overjoyed at the prospect of such an easy victory, sings his famous rondo. We've encountered that word "rondo" before in this course. When we listened to Mozart's "Non più andrai" from *The Marriage of Figaro*, I pointed out that it was a rondo. That means there was a refrain and the refrain kept coming back after various other verses. This is a rondo, and here is the refrain.

Farlaf: "The hour of my triumph approaches. My hated rival will go far away from us. O, knight, you are wasting your time in search of the princess. The witch's power will not let you get to her!" We'll keep hearing those words and the music associated with them interspersed between these next verses.

Lyudmila, your tears and groans are a waste of time, and you wait for your dear one in vain! Neither howls nor tears will do any good! Submit to Naina's power, princess!

Ruslan, forget about Lyudmila. Lyudmila, forget about Ruslan. At the very thought of possessing the princess my heart leaps with happiness, and I'm already beginning to feel the sweetness of revenge and love.

In travail, in anguish, annoyance, and sadness wander the world, my brave rival! Fight enemies, storm fortresses!

Without working or worrying, sitting in the castle of my forefathers, awaiting the commands of Naina the desired day approaches. The day of ecstasy and love!

Then we hear a reprise of three earlier heard verses, and this rondo ends. Note, please, the following: Farlaf is a bass and this aria demonstrates well the Russian preference for deep male voices, baritones and basses. Farlaf's aria combines an opera buffa-like patter with a distinctly Russian style of melody. Its melodic patterns are, of course, a reflection of the Russian language in which it is sung. That's the big reason why the melody sounds Russian, because of the natural declamatory rhythms of the Russian language.

Let's listen to this marvelous aria, a combination of Italian opera buffa-style patter and the rhythms and contours of Russian rhythm and Slavic melody.

(musical example)

One is reminded of Dr. Bartolo's aria, "*A un dottor della mia sorte,*" from Rossini's *Barber of Seville*. Here we have basically a criminal element, a bad guy, but a basso singing in such a comic patter that it's hard for us to take him really seriously as an evil person. He's more a comic cutout than anything else.

Ruslan himself is also a deep-voiced male, not the tenor we would expect in Italian opera, but rather a bass-baritone, that is, a male with a low voice that's used in the lowest end of his register. When Ruslan finally finds his beloved Lyudmila, she has been accursed. She's in a deep coma-like sleep and cannot be awakened. Ruslan's grief and frustration are well expressed in the following aria. "O love of my life, young wife!" He's jumping the gun a little there, but okay.

Can you really not hear me, the groans of your beloved? But her heart beats and flutters, and a smile plays on her beautiful lips. An unknown fear torments my soul! O, friends! Who knows whether her smile is for me, whether the heart beats for me?

Note the plaintive, lonely clarinet, which mirrors well Ruslan's isolation, which accompanies him in his grief; and please note that this is a baritone voice, not a basso, but he's using the baritone in the lower end of his range, which gives him a bass-like feel.

Ruslan's aria, "O love of my life," a most typical Russian romantic aria.

(musical example)

Glinka died in February of 1857. He did not just become a national hero; he was canonized, he was deified. "Beethoven and Glinka!" exclaimed Anton Rubinstein. Rubinstein's Russian contemporaries saw nothing exaggerated in this coupling. Among those who believed most fervently in Glinka's musical godhood was a young 20-year-old pianist and composer living in St. Petersburg, by the name of Mili Alekseyevich Balakirev. Balakirev lived from 1837 to 1910.

Balakirev and "The Five." Despite his minimal musical training, Balakirev set himself up as a music teacher and quickly became the czar of Russian music. What resulted when Balakirev put out his shingle and started gathering students remains one of the strangest things that has ever happened in music and could only have taken place in Russia in the mid-nineteenth century, with this huge talent pool and nowhere for that talent pool to go for training. I will let Harold Schonberg begin the story.

> Around Balakirev gathered a group of young musicians who were to become known as The Russian Five, a group of self-taught dilettantes active in other fields. Cesar Cui in 1856 was the first to be attracted to the Balakirev orbit. Cui, who was born in 1835 and died in 1918, was an army officer and remained one to the end of his life. He was an engineer and his specialty was fortifications. As a composer, he was the least talented of The Five. He was more valuable as a critic. His articles appeared in France as well as in Russia, and he

was constantly explaining the nationalistic principles of The Five.

Modest Mussorgsky, 1839 to 1881, was the next to enter the circle. He appeared to be an unlikely candidate for immortality. At that time, in 1857, he was an 18-year-old ensign in the crack Preobragzensky regiment and had been taught what every good regimental officer of the Preobragzensky had to know: how to drink, how to wench, how to wear clothes, how to gamble, how to flog a serf, and how to sit on a horse. Of this set of accomplishments Mussorgsky found drinking most congenial. His other big accomplishment was his ability to play the piano, his repertoire consisting of fashionable potpourris of the day.

Aleksander Borodin, then an army medical officer, met Mussorgsky in 1856 while both were duty officers at the same hospital. Borodin wrote of his first impression of Mussorgsky, "I had just been appointed an army doctor and Mussorgsky was a newly hatched officer. Being on hospital duty, we met in the common room, and feeling bored and in need of companionship we started talking and found each other most congenial. The same evening we were invited to the army doctor's house. Having a grown-up daughter he often gave parties to which the officers on duty were asked. Mussorgsky was at that time a very callow, most elegant, perfectly contrived little officer, carefully smoothed out, brand new, close-fitting uniform, toes well turned out, hair well oiled, hands shapely and well cared for. His manners were polished and aristocratic. He spoke through his teeth and his carefully chosen words were interspersed with French phrases and were rather labored. He showed, in fact, signs of slight pretentiousness, but also quite unmistakably a perfect breeding and education. He sat down at the piano and, coquettishly raising his hands, started playing delicately and gracefully, bits of *Trovatore* and *Traviata*, the circle around him rapturously murmuring '*Charmante*,' '*delicieux*.'" Charming. Delicious. Music was what Mussorgsky loved above all. So overwhelming was the impact of Balakirev upon him that Mussorgsky resigned his commission in 1857 and plunged madly into the study of music.

This is as far as we can go in this lecture. When we return for the next lecture, the remainder of The Five and how they came to know Balakirev; and then of course, we will focus specifically on Mussorgsky and his superb opera *Boris Godunov*.

Thank you.

Lecture Thirty—Transcript
Russian Opera, II

Welcome back to "How to Listen to and Understand Opera." This is Lecture 30, the second of a two-lecture set entitled "Russian Opera." Where we left off, we were talking about the accumulation of what we now call "The Russian Five." Balakirev is the teacher, the heart and soul of this group of young composers. The first to join Balakirev's circle was Cesar Cui, an army engineer. The second to join Balakirev's circle was Modest Mussorgsky, an army officer. We continue.

Into the Balakirev circle next came the young naval officer, Nicolai Rimsky-Korsakov, 1844 to 1908. Aleksander Borodin joined the Balakirev circle in 1862, and he is the fifth and last of what we call "The Five." Borodin's dates, 1833 to 1887. He was the illegitimate child of Prince Luka Gedianov. He was trained as a scientist and remained one his entire life. There they are, my friends, the army engineer, the ex-ensign, the naval cadet, and the chemist. This group of what were initially hobbyists changed the face of Russian music forever. Not since the Florentine Camerata has a group of dilettantes and semi-professionals had such a profound effect on the history of Western music.

Cesar Cui on the Russian "Mighty Handful;" Cui wrote so much about the group, and he describes their process of education. By the way, this phrase "Mighty Handful" is translated roughly into Russian—or should I say, the Russian that is translated into the "Mighty Handful" is "*Moguchaya Kuchka*." *Moguchaya Kuchka* means literally "The Magnificent Few," and we've translated that rather more gracefully into English as "The Mighty Handful," a handful being five. I read from Cui's reminiscence:

> We formed a close-knit group of young composers; and since there was nowhere to study, for us the Conservatory didn't exist, our self-education began. It consisted of playing through everything that had been written by all the greatest masters and all aspects were subjected to criticism and analysis in all their technical and creative aspects. We were young and our judgments were harsh.

I would add, they were also a little ignorant. I continue.

We were very disrespectful in our attitude toward Mozart and Mendelssohn. To the latter, we opposed Schumann, who we then ignored. We were very enthusiastic about Liszt and Berlioz and we worshipped Chopin and Glinka.

This is completely understandable; that they would worship nationalist composers of the highly expressive mid- and early-nineteenth century. I continue.

We carried on heated debates in the course of which we would down as many as four or five glasses of tea with jam. We discussed musical form, program music, vocal music and especially opera.

Their lack of schooling in traditional music theory forced The Five to discover their own way of doing things, and in the process, they called on the materials closest at hand, which were, my friends, folk songs. Their frequent use of actual or imitated folk material for generating themes in a work has literary parallels in the borrowings by Pushkin and Gogol of folktales as the basis of so many of their most characteristic stories.

Self-taught and proud of it, The Five made a virtue of their technical ignorance and raised the flag of their dogmatic nationalism at every opportunity. To The Five, the great enemies of Russian music were the Rubinstein brothers, Nicolai and Anton. Anton Rubinstein, pianist and composer, founded the St. Petersburg Conservatory in 1862. Nicolai Rubinstein, pianist, founded the Moscow Conservatory in 1864. For The Five, the Rubinsteins represented the Western European academic tradition and the ongoing threat of Western musical dominance over native Russian music. Cesar Cui wrote, "It would be a serious error to consider Anton Rubinstein a Russian composer. He is merely a Russian who composes." Balakirev considered the St. Petersburg Conservatory, and now I quote, "a plot to bring all Russian music under the yoke of the German generals."

Modest Mussorgsky wrote a letter to Rimsky-Korsakov dated August 15, 1868. I read that letter:

And another thing about German symphonic development. I tell you our cold *kvas* soup is a horror to the Germans and yet they eat it with pleasure. And their cold cherry soup is a horror to us and yet it sends a German into ecstasy. In short, symphonic development is just like German philosophy and soup, all worked out and systematized. When a German thinks, he reasons his way to a conclusion. Our Russian brother, on the other hand, starts with a conclusion and then might amuse himself with some reasoning. Just keep one thing in mind: The creative act carries within itself its own aesthetic laws. They're verification is inner criticism; their application is the artist's instinct. The artist is a law unto himself. When an artist revises it means he's dissatisfied. When he revises although satisfied, or worse, adds to what already satisfies, he is Germanizing, chewing over what has already been said. We Russians are not cud chewers. We are omnivores.

This is real *Moguchaya Kuchka* dogma. Say that five times, if you will.

It goes without saying that the academicians did not like The Five. For example, Tchaikovsky expressed his opinions regarding The Five in a letter dated January 5, 1878. Tchaikovsky's letter pretty much expresses what most educated Russian musicians thought of The Five, and I quote Tchaikovsky:

All the Petersburg composers are afflicted to the marrow with the worst sort of conceit and with a purely dilettantish confidence in their superiority over all the rest of the musical world. Cui is a dilettante. His music is devoid of originality. Borodin is a 50-year-old professor of chemistry at The Academy of Medicine. He has even less taste than Cui and his technique is so weak that he can't write a line without outside help. Mussorgsky is a has-been. In talent, he exceeds all the others but lacks the need for self-perfection. Balakirev has grown silent after accomplishing very little. He has gifts and they are lost because of some fateful circumstance that has made a saintly prig out of him. This, then, is my honest opinion of these gentlemen.

What a sad thing. With the exception of Rimsky-Korsakov, how many talents from whom it is futile to await anything worthwhile. Is this not generally the way in Russia, tremendous powers fatally hindered by a sort of Plevna from taking the field and joining battle as they should? Nevertheless, these powers exist. Even a Mussorgsky, by his very lack of discipline, speaks a new language. It is ugly, but it is also fresh...

Like it or not, a characteristically Russian music emerges from The Five, based on the model of Glinka—a music that employs Russian folk melodies or melodies created to sound like folk melodies; two, a music that is essentially thematic with little of the sort of development we would hear in German music; and three, a music that is rhythmically powerful, lyric, and often, to Western ears, emotionally unrefined.

Modest Petrovich Mussorgsky, 1839 to 1881. He's the first of The Five to compositionally mature. He's known for but a handful of works; sensational songs, my friends, his operas, *Boris Godunov* and *Khovanshchina*, and instrumental works such as the *Night on Bare Mountain* and *Pictures at an Exhibition*. Depression and alcohol led Mussorgsky to a very early death. Aleksander Borodin lamented Mussorgsky's downfall:

> This is horribly sad. Such a talented man and sinking so low. Now he periodically disappears then reappears, morose, untalkative, which is contrary to his usual habit. After a while, he comes to himself again, sweet, gay, amiable, and as witty as ever. Devil knows, what a pity.

Mussorgsky's great friend, the artist Ilya Repin, chronicled Mussorgsky's disintegration, and again I quote:

> It was really incredible how that well-bred guard's officer with his beautiful and polished manners, that witty conversationalist with the ladies, that inexhaustible punster, quickly sank, sold his belongings, even the elegant clothes, and soon descended to some cheap saloons where he personified the familiar type of the has-been, where this childishly happy child with a red, potato-shaped nose was already unrecognizable. Was it really he? The once impeccably dressed, heel-clicking society man, scented, dainty, fastidious? Oh, how many times our friend Stassov on his return from abroad was hardly able to get him out of some basement dive, nearly in rags, swollen with alcohol.

Mussorgsky died of a stroke on March 16th of 1881. He was only 42 years old.

Boris Godunov, story. The story takes place between 1598 and 1605 and is based on historical events. Boris Godunov is the chief minister and brother-in-law of Czar Feodor. For his own power-hungry ends, Boris arranges for the assassination of the heir to the throne, young Dmitri, the czar's half-brother. On the death of Czar Feodor, Boris has himself acclaimed by the people and ascends the throne. At about the same time, a young monk named Grigory leaves his monastery and goes to Poland, where he passes himself off as the dead czarevich, Dmitri. Are you still all with me? Let's continue. The Polish government puts this pretender at the head of a Polish army and marches against Russia. Russia is almost defenseless. Boris, plagued by guilt and nightmares over the assassination of the young Dmitri, is incapable of action. Boris dies and the former monk, Grigory, posing as Dmitri, ascends the throne and becomes czar.

My friends, there are six different versions of this opera. Quickly. Mussorgsky completed the original version in 1869, after 15 months of work. This version was rejected outright for performance. Mussorgsky's friends convinced him to rewrite the opera, which he did. He went so far as to add another whole act, the act we now know as the third act. This second version was completed in 1874. It was premiered that year and enjoyed modest success. It was performed 21 times before it disappeared from the repertoire in 1879.

After Mussorgsky died, his great friend Rimsky-Korsakov decided to rewrite *Boris* as a tribute to Mussorgsky. I quote Rimsky:

> I worship *Boris Godunov* and I hate it. I worship it for its originality, power, boldness, independence, and beauty. I hate it for its shortcomings, the roughness of its harmonies, the incoherence in the music. Although I know I shall be cursed for doing so, I will revise *Boris*. There are countless absurdities in its harmonies and at times its melodies. Unfortunately, Mussorgsky's followers will never understand.

Rimsky did a version in 1896, and then he did another version in 1908. This second Rimsky-Korsakov version, the fourth version of *Boris Godunov*, is the version typically heard today and the one which we will hear in just a moment. Not content, however, Karol Rathaus did another version, and Dmitri Shostakovich did a sixth version.

The structure of the opera consists of a prologue followed by four acts. In truth, it's a series of set pieces or what we would call "tableaux," each illuminating an episode from the life and death of Boris. Cesar Cui wrote of *Boris Godunov*:

> Each scene is independent. The roles for the greater part are transitory. The episodes necessarily have a certain connection, they all relate more or less to a common action, but the opera would not suffer from a rearrangement of the scenes or even from a substitution of certain secondary episodes by others. This is a result of the fact that *Boris*, properly speaking, is neither a drama nor an opera, but rather a musical chronicle after the manner of the historical dramas of Shakespeare.

Boris Godunov is based on a dramatic chronicle by Alexander Pushkin. Mussorgsky himself wrote the libretto. Central to Mussorgsky's libretto are two essential issues—one, the relationship between ruler and those who are ruled; and two, the corrupting influence of power. Lord Acton's famous comment applies well to Boris, "Power corrupts and absolute power corrupts absolutely." Great men are almost always bad men. Eric Plaut points out:

> The relationship between the hopelessly poor peasants and their all-powerful, frequently savage, and yet perennially vulnerable czars is a dominant theme in Russian history. With the prescience of genius, Mussorgsky chose a subject that continued to dominate Russia in the century after the opera was written. A nation so fearful of its foes that it found security in a dictatorial leader, a governmental process characterized by endless struggles for ascension to power and by government savagery in the name of law and order. Throughout the opera there are repeated references to the peoples' fear of the czar, his cruelty, his ruthlessness; yet Mussorgsky makes it quite clear that much as they fear a strong czar, the people fear being without a strong czar even more. Historically, the fear was well founded. Whenever Muscovite Russia had been without a strong ruler, she had been sacked repeatedly by Mongols, Poles, Tartars and Cossacks, her citizens slaughtered and sold into slavery. Only a powerful and ruthless czar had proven capable of

containing the nobility and its internecine warfare that led to national chaos.

No composer ever portrayed, as sympathetically as Mussorgsky did, the peasant class. Central to this sympathetic portrayal is Mussorgsky's attitude toward musical prosody, the accurate reproduction of Russian speech patterns in music. Again, I quote Mussorgsky:

> I should like to make my characters speak on the stage exactly as people do in real life, without exaggeration or distortion, and just write music that will be thoroughly artistic. What I project then is the melody of life. This is living prose in music. This is reference for the language of humanity. This is a reproduction of simple human speech. I want the notes to express exactly what the words express. I want truth.

My friends, Monteverdi could not have said it better himself.

Boris Godunov, the music. Prologue, 1598, Boris's ascension to the throne of Russia. Scene Two, about 15 minutes into the opera, an extraordinary contrast. The boyars, the Russian aristocrats ranked just below the ruling princes, have announced the ascension of Boris to an ecstatic populace. The boyars, "Long live Tsar Boris Feodorovich!" The people, "Long may he live! Like the radiant sun in the sky, Glory, glory! Glory, glory, glory to the Tsar, To Boris, the Tsar of Russia! Glory! Glory! Glory! Glory!" *"Slava! Slava! Slava! Slava!"* It's a magnificent and ecstatic celebration.

Then immediately, in stark contrast, a fearful Boris, filled with misgivings and guilt, prays for a successful rule.

> My soul is sad. Some sort of involuntary fear has gripped my heart with a sense of evil foreboding. Oh, Righteous One, oh sovereign Father of mine! Look down from the heaven on the tears of your faithful servants and send me a holy blessing for my rule: Let me be good and righteous as you are; may I rule my people in glory…Now let us pay our respects to the past rulers of Russia now deceased. And now invite the people to the feast, all from boyar to blind beggar, let everyone enter, you are all welcome!

Note please, the melodies are tinged with an absolutely Slavic Russian melodic sensibility. Note, two, that Boris is a bass—no surprise, again the Russian predilection for the bass voice; three, Mussorgsky's incredible prosody in Boris's aria. We have a syllabic setting fitted to the needs of the Russian language. We have the clarity of recitative and the melodic fluency and expressive power of aria.

(musical example)

It's quite magnificent, and again, quite Russian-sounding, as opposed to Italian, French or German music.

We move on to Varlaam's song. During the first act, we meet a drunken, old priest named Varlaam. He sings a raucous drinking song about the destruction of the Tatars at the hands of Czar Ivan the Terrible. Varlaam's song makes a very interesting contrast with Farlaf's rondo from Glinka's *Ruslan and Lyudmila*. Where Farlaf's song was clearly indebted to the patter aria style of Italian opera buffa, Varlaam's song has nothing to do with Italian opera. It is a rough, folkish, and, in its rhythms and prosody, thoroughly Russian song. I would read it to you now.

Varlaam:

> Here's what happened at the town of Kazan, Ivan the Terrible was feasting and making merry. He had given the Tatars a ruthless beating to teach them a lesson not to go wandering in Russia again. The Tsar came close, to the little town of Kazan. He dug some trenches under the river of Kazan. As the Tatars strolled about the town they stole glances at Tsar Ivan, those evil Tatars! Ivan the Terrible became sad, he hung his head on his right shoulder. The Tsar sent for all the gunners, the gunners with all their guns, the gunners with all their guns! A bright wax taper started smoking, a young gunner went up to the barrel. And the barrel of gunpowder started rolling. Help! It rolled along the trenches until it exploded. The evil Tatars shrieked and screamed, cursing in foul language. Hordes of Tatars fell, Forty-three thousand Tatars fell. That's what happened in Kazan…Ha, ha!

Varlaam's song. (musical example)

We move forward to Act Four, Scene Two, the death of Boris, one of the most moving scenes, really, in all of opera. Boris, who has hovered at the very edge of madness since the second act—and please remember it's the guilt over the execution of the young Dmitri that has caused this madness, this kind of feedback in Boris's mind. We now visit him at a moment of lucidity. As his death approaches, he calls for his son, Feodor, the czarevich. Boris says:

> Farewell, my son, I am dying…Now you will begin your reign. Do not ask me by what means I obtained the crown…You need not know. You will be a lawful ruler, as my successor, as my firstborn son…as my son! My dear child! Don't believe the slander of the seditious boyars, keep a sharp watch on their secret dealings with Lithuania. Punish treason harshly, punish without mercy; closely follow the judgment of the people, they are impartial; defend and guard the righteous faith, honour and respect the holy saints of the Lord.

I would tell you this next bit is exquisitely sweet and moving.

> Look after your sister, the Tsarevna, my son, you are now her only guardian…Our Xenia, the innocent dove.

Look, Boris's pain here is doubled. He knows that the Polish army with the pretender Grigory-Dmitri is approaching. Polish victory, seemingly inevitable at this point, will undoubtedly mean the death of his beloved children. In himself being responsible for the death of Dmitri, he has also now been responsible as he anticipates, for the death of his own.

> Oh Lord! Oh Lord! Look down I pray, upon the tears of a sinful father; I am not praying for myself, not for myself, my Lord! From you inaccessible height pour down your blessing light upon my children, my innocent…my sweet…pure children…Oh, heavenly powers! Guardians of the eternal throne…With your bright wings protect my dear child from all evils and calamity…from temptation…

At that moment, he hugs his son and kisses him. A long-sustained chime of a bell is heard. It is Boris's death knell and Boris is hearing it in his own mind. Boris says, "A bell! A knell!"

A chorus of monks sings from offstage; and again, this is all happening in Boris's mind. The monks are grieving for the dead czarevich, Dmitri. They're not grieving for Boris. "Weep, weep, oh people, there is no life in him any more, his lips are silent and he will never give an answer. Weep. Alleluia!" Then boyars and the chorus come onto the stage.

Boris says, "Funeral wails, the monastic order...The holy monastic order...The Tsar is joining the monks." The death knell continues underneath the voices. Feodor, Boris's son, says, "Your Majesty, calm down! The Lord will help..." Boris responds, "No! No, my son, my time has come..." Again, the chorus in Boris's mind sings of the dead czarevich, Dmitri. "I can see the dying child, and I weep and sob, he tosses and turns and calls for help, but nothing can save him..."

Boris yells out, "Oh Lord! Oh Lord! I feel terrible! There's nothing I can do now to atone for my sin! Oh evil death! How cruel are your torments!" He jumps up. "Wait! Wait! I am still Tsar!" But then he clutches his heart and falls into a chair. "I am still Tsar...Oh Lord! Death! Forgive me!" He points to his son. "Here, here is your Tsar...your Tsar...Forgive me..." In a whisper, "Forgive me..." The boyars in a whisper say, "He has died."

This is a three handkerchief or two-box of Kleenex section. Let's listen to the death of Boris.

(musical example)

Boris remains one of the really great tragic heroes in all of opera. We weep for him, even if he cannot weep for himself. Destroyed by his guilt over what he's done to gratify his lust for power, Boris in the end can neither save himself nor the lives of his children, and that's what's so touching about this last scene. It is his love for his children that comes through at the moment of his death. The power, the accoutrement, is meaningless to him. He just wants safety for his family, and it's the one thing he knows he cannot guarantee.

I would point out before my concluding remarks that the old divisions of recitative and aria are in Russian opera, almost from the beginning, inconsequential. If we hear recitative-like music it will always be accompanied by the orchestra, and I would point out the effortless ease with which Mussorgsky moves from recitative-like music through more melodic *arioso* to genuine aria and chorus and back again. Certainly the divisions of aria and recitative, that we talked about for so much of this course, have been pretty much done away with, the model of Verdi having much to do with that, by the 1850s and certainly by the 1860s.

Boris is a superb opera. It is the pinnacle of nineteenth-century Russian opera, a tradition begun but 38 years before with Glinka's *A Life for the Czar*. *Boris Godunov* is to nineteenth century Russian opera what Verdi's *Otello*, Wagner's *Tristan and Isolde*, and Bizet's *Carmen* are to nineteenth-century Italian, German and French opera—a spectacular culmination of what had come before, the best of its national type, and frankly, a very difficult if not impossible act for anyone else to follow. Thank you.

Lectures Thirty-One and Thirty-Two
Verismo, Puccini, and *Tosca*

Scope:

The finale lectures in this study of opera examine opera verismo: its origins, character, and greatest exponent—Giacomo Puccini. Puccini's virtues and faults are discussed—especially his marvelous power of lyricism, sometimes pursued at the expense of dramatic reality. The second act of his masterpiece, *Tosca*, is analyzed as a leading example of Puccini's style and as one of the most powerful acts in all opera. The study concludes with a musical illustration of the nature of opera, scene 9 from Richard Strauss's *Capriccio*. In essence opera is a whole that is greater than the parts.

Outline

I. Verismo opera.

    A. Verismo (truth) opera grew out of the 19th-century philosophical movements of positivism and naturalism.

        1. Positivism posits that the only reality that humankind should concern itself with is observable fact; there are no mysteries left in the world that science cannot explain.

        2. An offshoot of positivism is naturalism: the study of human relations.

        3. Realist/verismo authors and composers tend to depict the worlds of the criminal, the dispossessed, and the demoralized for their emotional extremes and for their absence of pose and artifice.

II. Giacomo Puccini (1858–1924).

    A. Puccini was the greatest composer of verismo operas. He was primarily a man of the theater. He wrote twelve operas, three of which remain among the most popular in the repertory: *Tosca*, *La Bohème*, and *Madame Butterfly*.

    B. Puccini was born in Lucca in 1858, the last in a five-generation line of respected musicians.

        1. He studied at the Milan Conservatory with Amilcare Ponchielli.

        2. His first huge success was *La Bohème* of 1896.

        3. Puccini was not an innovator. As a composer he was not controversial. Unlike Verdi, Puccini did not constantly evolve, seeking ever-greater drama and movement in his operas. He was, however, a superb and sympathetic melodist, whose other compositional skills were brought to bear directly on the dramatic materials before him: stage action, impulsive feeling, and truth in expression— often exaggerated expression.

III. The Puccinian dilemma.

    A. Many important critics, composers, and music historians of today have dismissed Puccini as an artless hack. They have backed up their criticisms with sound arguments regarding Puccini's compositional technique and the content and nature of his libretti.

    B. Opera in Italy has almost always been a popular entertainment. Puccini's operas are very much part of this tradition.

IV. *Tosca* (1900).

    A. The large outline of the story is based on historical events surrounding the "liberation" of Rome by Napoleonic forces around 1800.

    B. Act 1 introduces us to the characters.

        1. Mario Cavaradossi (tenor) is the hero and lover of

        2. Floria Tosca, a hot-blooded, beautiful opera singer.

        3. Cesare Angelotti is a nationalist and freedom-fighter who has just escaped from prison.

        4. Vitellio Scarpia is the evil and sadistic chief of the secret police.

    C. Act 2 is one of the greatest of all Puccini's operatic acts and the focal point in this opera.

        1. Scarpia desires Tosca and will use her to find Angelotti. Scarpia's aria ("Ella verrà …") demonstrates effortless vocal lyricism at the expense of dramatic reality. Scarpia could sound more evil than he does. This is the kind of thing that has put *Tosca* under fire from critics. Also noteworthy is Puccini's melding of parlante, arias, etc. into a continuous flow of music. Musical example: Act 2 from Scarpia's "Tosca è un buon falco!" to the end of Scarpia's aria, "Ella verrà …"

2. Scarpia tries to discover where Angelotti is hiding by questioning Cavaradossi, who resists him. Musical example: "Ov'è Angelotti?"
3. The questioning turns ugly.
4. Tosca enters. In her presence, Scarpia has Cavaradossi tortured in an adjoining room. This scene of brutal torture is unique in opera. Puccini piles on the agony to a climax of unbearable tension. Its depiction of the worst of human behavior is typical of verismo.
5. Tosca cannot bear her psychological torture any longer. She tells Scarpia where Angelotti is hiding. Scarpia orders the end of Cavaradossi's torture. Musical example: torture scene from Scarpia's "Orsù, Tosca, parlate" to his "Portatelo qui"
6. Cavaradossi learns of Napoleon's victory at Marengo. He revives and sings a victory song. Scarpia orders him to the gallows and forbids Tosca to accompany him. Puccini continues to pile one climactic moment upon the next. Musical example: Cavaradossi's "Vittoriá!" to Scarpia's "Voi noi"
7. Tosca tries to negotiate for Cavaradossi's life. Scarpia reveals that the price is Tosca herself. Musical example: Tosca's "Quanto?" through Scarpia's "Già. Mi dicon venal"
8. Tosca is repelled and feels that God has abandonned her. She sings one of Puccini's most beloved and famous arias, "Vissi d'arte" (musical example).
9. Tosca agrees to yield to Scarpia in exchange for Cavaradossi's life and a safe-conduct pass. Scarpia appears to agree to her request. He writes the pass, but when he tries to embrace her, she plunges a knife into him and kills him. Musical example: Scarpia's "Io tenni la promessa" to the end of the scene

D. Puccini's operas exhibit a wonderful balance of words and music. His stories are dramatically compelling, and his balance of words and music heightens and deepens the dramatic meaning and expressive content.

V. Course conclusion.

A. Richard Strauss's last opera, *Capriccio* (1941), has the last word.

1. *Capriccio* takes place outside Paris around 1775, at a time when Gluck's operatic reforms were raising a storm of discussion and controversy.
2. *Capriccio* is an opera about opera, particularly about the relationship between words and music.
3. In one scene a poet, composer and a stage director argue the relative merits of their respective crafts. Musical example: scene 9 from *Capriccio*

B. Is opera words or music? It is neither. It is an indefinable combination of both. The whole is always greater than the parts.

Lecture Thirty-One—Transcript
Verismo, Puccini, and *Tosca*, I

Welcome to "How to Listen to and Understand Opera." This, my friends, is Lecture 31, the first of a two-lecture set entitled "Verismo, Puccini and *Tosca*." First, verismo opera definitions. Through the second half of the nineteenth century, Italian and French writers and opera composers sought to capture ever greater dramatic truth in their works. This meant portraying people, events, and emotions with ever greater accuracy, without the sort of artifice we hear in Meyerbeer's *The Huguenots* or for that matter in Rossini's *The Barber of Seville*. Bizet's *Carmen*, Verdi's *Otello*, and the works of the writer Emil Zola, for example, shoot from the emotional hip. They all portray real people in profoundly weakened and often degraded emotional states, struggling for their very survival as human beings. This move toward stark, dramatic, and expressive realism is called in opera in Italy *verismo*, meaning simply truth or, even more accurately, truthism.

The textbooks will tell us that verismo opera grew out of a nineteenth-century philosophy called "positivism." Bear with me for a moment while we go through these isms and dogma, and in doing so seek the greater truth and apply it to the opera of late nineteenth-century Italy. In any case, the textbooks tell us that verismo opera grew out of a nineteenth-century philosophy called "positivism." Positivism posits that personkind had outgrown theology and metaphysics, that the only reality one should concern oneself with was observable fact. Positivism assumed that there were no mysteries left in the world that science could not explain.

A mid-nineteenth century offshoot of positivism was a philosophical and artistic movement called "naturalism." So an offshoot of this positivism, which is a very intellectual look at the world, is a movement called "naturalism." The object of naturalism was to understand logically and scientifically the essence of human society, that is, human relationships, human interaction, how human society functioned and what the effects of society were on individual people. According to Emil Zola, naturalism was "The formulas of modern science," that is positivism, "applied to literature." David Kimbell writes:

> Like realism, naturalism tended to concentrate its attentions on areas socially neglected by earlier literary movements:

lowlife, the criminal, the dispossessed, the demoralized. In some measure this was due to the political tendency of this movement, but there was also an artistic reason for this choice of celebrating and examining the dispossessed, the criminal, the lowlife. The realists looked to such worlds for simplicity, for authenticity, for the absence of pose and artifice. The naturalist preferred them, that is the lowlife, the dispossessed, the criminals, because the relationship between society and its victims was much more interesting than the relationship between society and successful men and women.

My friends, we are still positive naturalists today in this way. If we turn on the TV set, we are much more likely to see a television show about criminals, about cops, about hospitals that celebrate the victimized and dispossessed, than we are likely to see a TV show about a wealthy, happy, philanthropic financier. People who have already made their way in the world are not as interesting as those who are not making their way in the world; and so naturalism, verismo, positivism all celebrate the underside of human society, and this is what so many writers in France and Italy were interested in as we move toward the close of the nineteenth century.

In Italy, according to the textbooks, operatic naturalism, realism or verismo, began with Pietro Mascagni's opera *Cavalleria Rusticana* in 1890 and Ruggero Leoncavallo's *I Pagliacci* in 1892. All right, this might be what the textbooks say, that *verismo* opera begins in 1890; but in reality, if you'll excuse me, Italian operatic verismo had existed since at least Verdi's *La Traviata* of 1853—real people, real situations, real victims, real illness.

The great operatic exponent of Italian verismo opera was Giacomo Antonio Domenico Michele Secondo Maria Puccini. According to Robert Donington, "Puccini is much the best of verismo and *Tosca* may well be the best of Puccini." Giacomo Puccini, 1858 to 1924. Not long before he died, Puccini wrote to a friend, "Almighty God touched me with his little finger and said, 'Write for the theater, mind, only for the theater,' and I have obeyed that supreme command." Puccini once described himself—quite accurately, apparently—as, and again I quote, "A mighty hunter of wild fowl, opera libretti, and attractive women."

Puccini's career would seem to be, if not a short one, then at least constrained by not that many operas. He only wrote 12 operas in total. Three of them are one-act operas designed to be performed together; that is the work *Il Trittico*. One of these 12 operas, *Turandot*, was left incomplete at the time of his death. Yet, three of Puccini's operas remain really among, if not the, most popular in the repertoire. They are of course, *Tosca*, *La Bohème*, and *Madame Butterfly*, with *Turandot* and *Manon Lescaut* not far behind.

Puccini's life can be outlined fairly quickly. He was born in Lucca on December 22nd of 1858, literally in the shadow of Verdi. I can't resist pointing out a wonderful bit of trivia. December 22nd of 1808 was the night of this incredible concert in Vienna, the night that Beethoven premiered his Fifth and Sixth Symphonies, re-performed the Fourth Piano Concerto, and introduced any other number of very important pieces in a four-hour long concert in a freezing cold recital hall. Puccini was born on the 50th anniversary of that incredibly auspicious evening in Beethoven's life. It's an absolutely useless detail, but such details, of course, are what make life worth living.

Puccini was the last, as it turned out, of a line of five generations of respected musicians. Puccinis had been professional musicians in Lucca since 1712. This was a family thing. It was understood that a Puccini son would be musical, would be trained in music and would likely become a professional musician. He was apparently a lazy, indifferent student. One of his teachers reported, "He comes to school only to wear out the seat of his pants." I would not be very satisfied if one of my children brought that back on his or her report card, but this is just how Puccini was. Whether he was lazy or indifferent is unimportant. He was good enough musically to be accepted and to attend the Milan Conservatory of Music. This is that same Milan Conservatory that rejected Verdi. Certainly, as a young man Puccini's "chops" were adequate to move on to the higher level of musical education that a conservatory would offer. His main teacher at the conservatory was Amilcare Ponchielli, who was the composer of *La Giocanda, I Lituani*, and a host of other popular late nineteenth-century Italian operas. Puccini's first opera was *Le Villi* of 1884. He was 26 years old. Puccini's first huge success, and indeed, the opera that made him both rich and famous, was *La Bohème*. It was written in 1896 when Puccini was 38 years old.

Puccini is to Verdi what Strauss was to Richard Wagner, the successor who could not possibly top his role model. Sometimes I think we expect much too much of Puccini. How could anyone be expected to walk in the footsteps of Verdi? Puccini was not an innovator, but even across the span of his career we see no great difference in his last opera, *Turandot*, than we see in his first great successful work, *La Bohème*, whereas Verdi, of course, evolved constantly, forever seeking greater drama and greater movement. Puccini was not controversial. Puccini was apolitical. He was not particularly interested in the musical scene around him. Puccini was, as he told us at the very beginning of this lecture, a man of the theater, period, exclamation mark. So, let us please take Puccini at face value. He was a superb and sympathetic melodist who brought his other compositional skills to bear directly on the dramatic necessities before him, stage action, impulsive feeling, and truth in expression, verismo in expression.

Before we move on we've got to talk about what I would call "the Puccinian dilemma." Many important critics, composers, and music historians have not been willing to take Puccini at face value. *Tosca*, 1900, for example, has taken some major critical hits over the years. This would seem not to be a terribly big deal. Lots of the operas that we've listened to across the span of this course were received poorly, or at least received not as we receive them today, at their premieres. They were not all big hits from the very beginning; but almost one hundred years after its premiere, *Tosca* and indeed Puccini himself continue to be assailed by some composers and some critics, despite the fact that they have been the mainstay of the repertoire since their creation.

This is a very unusual state of affairs, my friends, that operas that have been intrinsic and core repertoire would be, 100 years later, questioned ever more by composers and critics. Usually it's the other way around, the critics abuse a piece at its premiere, it survives 100 years, and then everyone embraces it as having been intrinsic to its age, whether the contemporaries acknowledged it or not. The other way around, these pieces have been central repertoire and are now being abused, this is "the Puccinian dilemma." I would read you some fairly contemporary critical response toward Puccini. According to critic Harold Schonberg, who for many years was the chief critic for the *New York Times*, "The Puccini operas may be naïve, and musicians have accused them of pandering to a listener's baser instincts. There's no denying that many Puccini operas are frank tear-jerkers, and those who regard opera as an art of spiritual betterment reject them out of hand."

According to composer Arnold Schonberg, no relation, please, "There are higher and lower means of artistic expression. Realistic violent incidents, as for example, the torture scene in the second act of *Tosca*, which are unfailingly effective, should not be used by an artist because they are too cheap, too accessible to everybody."

According to composer Benjamin Britten, who wrote marvelous operas himself, "I am sickened by the cheapness and emptiness of Puccini's music." There, twice we're heard that word "cheap," and we're not talking about birdsong here.

According to the ordinarily unassailable musicologist Joseph Kerman:

> The more fully one knows the true achievement of the art of opera the more clearly one sees the extent of Puccini's failure as an opera composer, or more correctly, the triviality of his attempt. *Tosca*, for example, is consistently throughout of café music banality. It is scarcely believable that such an opera could have become a favorite. *Tosca* is a shabby little shocker.

Well, my goodness! Great composers and great musicologists alike have trashed Puccini and *Tosca*, flushed both the composer and his opera down the toilet of taste into the Tiber. Oh my, oh my. Why then am I presenting this composer, this opera, to you, my dear friends and listeners? Because, and heaven help me, my poor simple soul, I'm crazy about *Tosca*. Color me cheap, color me easy, an operatic slut, fine; I can live with all of that, but I cannot live without Puccini, and particularly, I will not live without *Tosca*. It's a necessary pleasure, if perhaps a guilty one.

I'll be straight with you. If *Tosca's* saccharine, sweet melodies, melodramatic duets, sadomasochistic scenes of torture and date rape don't tear out your heart and stomp on it and make you weep like an idiot, then one, you are simply too smart for the rest of us; two, your sophistication has developed to a point where you are no longer capable of appreciating the basic things in life, like a great chili dog, a sloppy kiss, a perfectly executed double-play or a '57 Chevy convertible. I mean, do we deny ourselves ice cream because it's fattening? Do we not drink martinis because they have alcohol? And thirdly, if this opera "don't tear out your heart and stomp on it," you are no longer able to kick back, let it hang, and just have a good old time. To Puccini's and *Tosca's* critics I say, "Lighten up! Let it go, man! Let it go! Wallow in the fat, just for the cheap, bloody hell of it!" And there, I used the word "cheap" too.

As we should all know by now, opera has almost always been a popular entertainment in Italy, so why shouldn't late nineteenth-, early twentieth-century Italian opera à la Puccini be an essentially popular art? Well, popular art it is, but all that is popular is not necessarily kitsch and all that is kitsch is not necessarily bad. So let us enjoy, celebrate, and revel in, indeed submerge ourselves in the glorious soap opera that is Puccini's *Tosca*. I feel much better now. Thank you very much.

Tosca, 1900. The action takes place in Rome. The large outline of the story is based on historical events. In the wake of the French Revolution, which began in 1789, a spirit of freedom and nationalism sweeps across the Italian peninsula. The French, seen as liberators, march on Rome in 1798. The French established a Roman republic in Rome and this is where the *Tosca* story kicks in. Cesare Angelotti is assigned as one of the governors of Rome, one of the two co-governing consuls. The combined forces of Britain, Austria, and Russia drive the French out of Rome. A brutal secret police force is created to keep order in the city, and this police force is headed by the evil Baron Vitellio Scarpia. We have a job and here's the job for all of us; every time I mention the name Scarpia you must hiss quietly, as Europeans would. *Sssss*. And I will play the music that is associated with Scarpia (piano example). This is the Scarpian leitmotif that represents all that is bad, low, and evil in this opera; and if nothing else, you will know it quite by heart by the time we finish our exploration of *Tosca*. I'm testing you—Scarpia! *Ssss*. (piano example) Very good.

Cesare Angelotti, one of those two consuls appointed by the French liberators, has been imprisoned for treason against the State. The action of the opera takes place against this background, over the course of a single day in June of 1800. The curtain rises on Act One just as Angelotti has escaped from the prison in the Castel Sant'Angelo.

The dramatic structure of the opera. The libretto is by Giuseppe Giacosa and Luigi Illica. By the way, Giacosa and Illica together with Puccini, were know in their day as "The Holy Trinity." Everything they touched turned to gold, or perhaps we should say to *lire*. This opera is based on the play, *La Tosca*, by Victorien Sardou, a French playwright very taken with realism and naturalism. It's a typical three-act structure. Act One, we meet the characters and the dramatic situation. Act Two, the action, and I will tell you now what we're going to do when we begin exploring this opera is we're going to listen to the great bulk of Act Two. I will read as much of the libretto as time allows me to read; but it's Act Two where the action takes place that really should be the focal point of our attention and so it shall be. Act Three is the denouement, the moment of truth when all the loose strings are tied together and revelation occurs. It is the response to the action of Act Two.

Quickly, let me outline what happens in Act One. We can't do Act Two without knowing what preceded it. The action takes place in the church of Sant'Andrea della Valle. The painter and masculine tenor/hunk/hero, Mario Cavaradossi, is painting from memory a portrait of a beautiful young woman that he has seen in the church. Enter Cesare Angelotti, who has just escaped. He lets himself into the family chapel with a key that's been left behind by his sister. The woman that Cavaradossi has painted turns out to be Angelotti's sister, who has left behind, in the family chapel, food and a disguise for her brother. The jailbreak has obviously been well planned.

Cavaradossi and Angelotti meet, and Cavaradossi offers to hide Angelotti in a well on the grounds of his, Cavaradossi's, villa. Cavaradossi gets involved right away. He shouldn't be, but he involves himself. Enter Floria Tosca, Angelotti's heart-throb. She is a beautiful, passionate, talented singer of great popularity and fame. She is also the object of the evil Scarpia's desire. *Sssss.* (piano example) Bravo.

Scarpia enters the church. Cavaradossi has just departed so their paths do not cross. Scarpia enters in search of Angelotti. Scarpia immediately recognizes Angelotti's sister in Cavaradossi's painting, which is still sitting on an easel in the church; and then Scarpia discovers Angelotti's discarded disguise, the disguise that he didn't need because he was going to go hide in the well of Cavaradossi's house.

Scarpia's not a dumb man, and he puts *due e due* together and he realizes that Cavaradossi is in some way involved with Angelotti's escape. "Bravissimo," thinks Scarpia. *Sssss.* (piano example) I'll stop doing that soon, but not quite yet. "Bravissimo," thinks Scarpia as he contemplates the execution of Cavaradossi and even more important, the taking of Tosca.

That brings us to Act Two, one of the greatest of all Puccini's operatic acts. We begin at the beginning with Scarpia's plan of action and his credo. Please, let us read the libretto. The action takes place in the Farnese Palace, Scarpia's room on the upper floor. The table is laid for supper. A large window gives onto the courtyard of the Palace. It is night. Scarpia is sitting at the table, having supper. From time to time he interrupts his meal to reflect. He takes a watch from his pocket, and in his restless demeanor, he betrays a feverish anxiety. He begins in recitative but, of course, no longer will we hear dry recitative, since the mid nineteenth century, since both Verdi and Wagner proved that continuous drama is infinitely more interesting than the old divisions of aria and recitative. We will not hear those divisions any longer, so we should not expect any moment when the orchestra will not be playing in this opera.

"Tosca is a good decoy! By now my bloodhounds must have sunk their teeth into their two quarries! Tomorrow's dawn will see Angelotti and the handsome Mario hanging on the gallows." Ha, ha, ha, ha. He rings a handbell. Sciarrone appears. Sciarrone is one of his henchmen.

"Is Tosca in the palace?" Sciarrone says, "A footman has just gone to fetch her." Scarpia, pointing to the window, "Open it. The hour is late." From the lower floor, where the Queen of Naples, Maria Carolina, is giving a great entertainment in honor of General Melas, is heard the sound of an orchestra. As the window is opened, the orchestra has to play kind of like they're in the distance. This is the orchestra of the party going on at a lower floor of the palace.

Now quickly, I have to explain some historical stuff. The Queen of Naples, Maria Carolina, would be an enemy of the French and an enemy of the French Revolution. General Melas is the general that has just been given credit for having defeated the Napoleonic forces and re-liberated the already liberated Rome. It's hard to keep track of who's on what side here. Just suffice to say for now that the French were perceived across the European continent, in the days before

Napoleon made himself emperor, as the liberators who would liberate Europe from the abject power of the absolute monarchs that had ruled for so many hundreds and hundreds of years. Despite the fact that the Italians are controlling Italy right now, those Italians are seen as oppressive because they represent a repressive monarchial system. Anyway, there's a party going on downstairs celebrating General Melas who has supposedly defeated the French forces and reinstated the power of Maria Carolina.

In any case, Scarpia hears this music and says, "The diva is not here yet for the cantata," so clearly she's coming in to sing. "And they're filling in with gavottes." We're going to hear these old gavotte dances being played in the background. Now everything will be *parlante*, and it's really hip. What we've got in the background is this old dance music, these gavottes played by the orchestra, and everything Scarpia says now will be layered on top, *parlante* style, of the gavotte. This is something that Verdi showed us all how to do, and any other composer of Italian opera would be a fool, if not quite crazy, not to do the same thing.

Scarpia turns to Sciarrone, "You will wait for Tosca at the entrance and tell her that I expect her when the cantata is over...or still better..." He hurriedly writes a note. "You will give her this note." Sciarrone goes out. Scarpia returns to the table and pours himself a drink. "She will come....for the love of her Mario! For love of her Mario she will submit to my pleasure." At that moment we hear, no surprise. (piano example) We know his pleasure is bad news. "The depth of her misery will match the depth of her love." Now we hear Scarpia's credo, a genuine aria where he lays out who he is, what he is, what he wants, and how he intends to get it.

> She will come for love of Mario. A forcible conquest has a keener relish than a willing surrender. I find no delight in sighs and sentimental moonlight serenades. I cannot thrum chords on a guitar, nor tell fortunes from flower petals, nor make sheep's-eyes or coo like a turtledove! I have strong desires. I pursue what I desire, glut myself with it and discard it, turning to a new diversion. God created different beauties and different wines. I wish to savor all I can of what heaven produces!

Let us listen to this entire opening; and let me point out the following before we do. Note please, the effortless movement back and forth between recitative, *parlante, arioso* and aria, as well as the pastiche, that is, the pasting in of this old gavotte in the background while we hear parlante stacked on top of it. After Verdi, all Italian operatic music is continuous and this continuity is very well wrought in this scene.

(musical example)

I would also point out the effortless lyricism of this passage. However, some of this lyricism, and we can be slightly critical without dissing our friend Puccini too much, this effortless lyricism may be at the expense of character development. What I mean by that is this: Scarpia could certainly have sounded meaner and rottener, like Iago in his credo in Verdi's *Otello*, where really the darkness of Iago's character is revealed; that doesn't happen here. Puccini would rather maintain a wonderful, broad, and passionate lyricism. Although I would tell you, by act's end the repulsive character of Scarpia will be well revealed musically. These are the kind of things that have put *Tosca* under fire from critics, that we have a bad guy singing about his lusts and desires and he doesn't sound all that bad, because in cases like this Puccini may very often err on the side of being overly lyric rather than being dramatic.

It has been pointed out that grand opera is filled with nasty villains, but even in the company of such sadists as Mephistopheles and Iago, Scarpia is unique, for his sadism is overtly sexual. To make sure we are fully clear that Scarpia is a sexual sadist, Puccini and his librettists have Scarpia say so three times. The first time he says it here, "A forcible conquest has a keener relish than a willing surrender." Later he says to Tosca, "Your eyes which darted hatred at me made my desire all the more fierce," and later than that he says, "How you hate me! This is how I want you." He's not a likeable human being.

The second part of Act Two: The police report comes in. Sciarrone enters and says, "Spoletta is here." Spoletta is another one of Scarpia's henchmen. Scarpia, "Send him in. It's about time." Scarpia sits back down, intent on his supper, and interrogates Spoletta without looking at him.

"Well my fine fellow. How went the chase?" Spoletta, "St. Ignatius, help me please. We followed the trail of the lady, when we arrived at a remote little villa hidden among the thickets, she went in." He's telling Scarpia that they followed Tosca and Tosca went to Cavaradossi's little villa, and she went inside the villa. What this means is that Tosca has got to know whatever Cavaradossi's involvement is, what that involvement is, and Tosca might even know where Angelotti is.

"When we arrived in a remote little villa hidden among the thickets she went in but quite soon came out again alone. Then with my colleagues I quickly scaled the garden wall and stormed the house." Scarpia, "Well done, Spoletta." Spoletta, "We hunted, we ransacked, we ferreted..." "And Angelotti?" "Wasn't to be found."

Scarpia, oh he's mad, "You dog! You traitor! You bungling idiot! To the gallows!" Spoletta, "Merciful Jesus. The painter was there." "Cavaradossi?" "He knows where the other's hidden. His every gesture, his every word exhibited such mocking irony that I put him under arrest."

Now Scarpia is feeling much better about things. "Ha, ha. That's better." Spoletta, pointing to the anteroom, "He's in there." Scarpia paces up and down thoughtfully. Suddenly he stops, as through the open window we hear the singers; we know now that Tosca is in the building. Scarpia, struck by an idea, suddenly says to Spoletta, "Bring in the cavaliere, and fetch Roberti and the judge of the exchequer." Spoletta and three police-agents lead in Cavaradossi. Then enter Roberti, the torturer, the judge of the exchequer with a clerk, and Sciarrone. The torturer is there.

Let's continue the questioning of Cavaradossi. All of this is done *parlante* and is done quite brilliantly. Of course, Cavaradossi, a nobleman, is outraged at being hauled in for no particular reason, and that's the first thing he says, "This is an outrage." Scarpia, with studied courtesy, "Cavaliere, please be seated." "I want to know..." "Please sit down." "I'll stand!"

Scarpia says, "As you wish. You know that the prisoner escaped today from the Castel Sant'Angelo?" Cavaradossi responds, "How should I know?" Scarpia: "Yet it is alleged that you sheltered him in Sant'Andrea, provided him food and clothing." "It's a lie!" "And led him to a farm of yours outside the city." "I deny it! What evidence have you?" Scarpia: "A faithful subject."

Cavaradossi responds, "Come to the point. Who has accused me? Your spies searched my villa in vain." Scarpia says, "Proof that he was well hidden." Cavaradossi: "Mere police suspicion." Spoletta: "Yes. He laughed at our searches." Cavaradossi responds, "And I still laugh." He's filled with bravado. "Ha, ha, ha, ha." Scarpia responds, "You'll find this no place for laughter. I warn you, enough now. Reply." Irritated and disturbed, he closes the window; he doesn't even want to hear the singers any more.

The interrogation of Cavaradossi turns ugly, and this we will listen to. It is a superb and powerful passage of great action and great impact. Scarpia barks out, "Where is Angelotti?" Cavaradossi, he is heroic. He is a tenor and a quite dramatic one. "I don't know." Scarpia: "Do you deny having given him food?" "I do!" "And the clothes?" "I deny it." Scarpia: "And sheltering him in your villa? And that he is hidden there?" "I deny everything." "*Nego! Nego!*"

Scarpia: "Come Cavaliere, reflect: this obstinacy of yours is unwise. Prompt confession could save you much anguish. I advise you to tell me: where is Angelotti?" "I don't know." "Once more and for the last time: where is he?" "I don't know!" Spoletta, aside: "Now the cords will be tightened!" At this moment, enter Tosca, anxiously. Scarpia says, "Ah, there she is!"

Tosca, seeing Cavaradossi, runs to embrace him. "Mario, you here?"Cavaradossi says under his breath, "Say nothing of what you have seen there, or it will mean my death!" So Tosca knows. Tosca knows where Angelotti is and, of course, she's been warned to say nothing about it. CavaradossI: "…or it will mean my death." Scarpia: "Mario Cavaradossi, the judge is waiting to take your deposition." He says to the torturer, "First the usual way. Afterwards…as I indicate." The judge goes into the torture chamber; the others follow, leaving Tosca and Scarpia alone. Spoletta withdraws to the door at the back of the room.

We will listen to the second half of the interrogation from where Scarpia says, "Where is Angelotti?"

(musical example)

All right, my friends, the gang's all there. This is what Scarpia has been waiting for. He's got Mario Cavaradossi in a side room, a torture chamber where the torturer is prepared to take his confession. He's got Tosca in his room with him, and now the machinations begin. Scarpia decides it's time to have a little chat with Tosca.

Scarpia says, "And now, let us have a friendly chat. There's no need to feel alarmed." Tosca, seating herself with affected calm, "I'm not alarmed." Scarpia, at first, my friends, is all congeniality, but slowly he begins his interrogation of a clearly frightened Tosca. Even as they chat, Cavaradossi's torture is being prepared in the adjacent room. She hasn't a clue of what's going on.

The torture of Cavaradossi I've divided into two parts. I would read the first part now, we will take our break, and then come back and read and listen to the second part.

Scarpia: "Sciarrone, what does the cavaliere say?" Yes, the true ugliness begins. Sciarrone, appearing in the doorway, "He says nothing." Scarpia: "Then let us insist." Sciarrone goes back inside shutting the door.

Tosca says, "This is useless." Scarpia: "We shall see, dear lady." Tosca: "So to satisfy you I must tell you lies?" Scarpia: "No, but the truth could shorten a very painful hour for him." Tosca is alarmed all of a sudden, "A painful hour? What do you mean? What is happening in that room?"

She has not been particularly quick on the uptake. She can't believe that this is happening. Scarpia: "The law is being enforced." Tosca: "Oh God! How?" Scarpia: "Bound hand and foot, your lover has around his temples a circlet of steel, which at each denial mercilessly makes blood gush forth." Tosca: "It's not true! It's not true! It's a diabolical jest. Have mercy, Scarpia!" "It lies in your power to save him." Tosca: "Well then, but stop, stop them!"

Scarpia: "Loosen him." Sciarrone says, "Entirely?" Scarpia says, "Yes, entirely." He turns to Tosca. "And now, the truth." Tosca says, "Let me see him." Scarpia says, "No!" Tosca says, "Mario!" She screams his name and from the closed door we hear Cavaradossi's voice, "Tosca!" Tosca says, "Are they still torturing you?" Cavaradossi's voice, "No. Have courage. Be silent. I scorn pain."

My goodness! What a stud! We'll see how much pain he can scorn as we move into the second and really brutal part of this scene. Let's take our break and when we come back, the torture of Cavaradossi and Tosca.

Thank you.

Lecture Thirty-Two—Transcript
Verismo, Puccini, and *Tosca*, II

Welcome back to "How to Listen to and Understand Opera." This is our final lecture, Lecture 32, the second of a two-lecture set entitled "Verismo, Puccini and *Tosca*." We return at really the dramatic crux of this terrifying and brutal second act, the second part of the torture of Cavaradossi, where the torture becomes the torture of Tosca as well. I read from the libretto.

Scarpia: "And now, Tosca, speak out." Tosca says, "I know nothing!" Scarpia: "That test was not enough? Roberti, repeat the treatment..." And, of course, Roberti is the torturer and this means more of the same. Tosca: "No! Stop!" Scarpia: "Will you speak?" Tosca: "No...you monster! You are torturing him, you're killing him!"

These are very dramatic words, my friends; these are terrifying words. I would point out that despite the brutality of these words, we hear an almost Neapolitan song-like musical substance. Again, we can criticize Puccini for that, but the violence is there, the action is there, the pathos is there; he is simply speaking in a very lyric language. His accusers would call him base and cheap. I call it "Puccini." Let's continue, please.

Scarpia: "That silence of yours is harming him far more." Tosca: "You laugh? You laugh...at this terrible suffering?" Scarpia: "Tosca was never more tragic on the stage! Open the doors so that she can hear his cries!" To drive it home even more, they open the doors to the torture chamber so that now all of the noise can come right into the room where Tosca and Scarpia are. Spoletta opens the door, placing himself directly in front of it.

Cavaradossi's voice cuts through, "I defy you!" Scarpia: " Harder, harder!" Cavaradossi's voice: "I defy you!!" Scarpia: "Speak!" Tosca says, "What can I say?" Scarpia: "Come, quickly!" Tosca: "I know nothing! Must I tell lies?" Scarpia again insists, "Say where Angelotti is! Speak out now! Where is he hidden?"

Tosca reaches a climax of grief, "Ah! I cannot bear it! Cease this torment! It is too much to suffer!" At this moment she sings this impassioned and extremely lyric musical line that goes like this, (piano example) at the very top of her range; and we feel her pain. It's a climactic moment because we realize that there are truly two people being tortured right now. It's not just Cavaradossi. The emotional and mental pain that Tosca is feeling is bringing her to the breaking point as well.

She says, "I cannot bear it!" Cavaradossi's voice cuts through the air, "Ahhhh!" This agonized scream. Tosca again turns imploringly to Scarpia, who signs to Spoletta to let her approach. She goes to the open door and, terrified at the sight of the dreadful scene, addresses Cavaradossi. So now she's not just hearing him, she's looking at him out there on the rack.

Tosca: "Mario, will you let me speak?" Cavaradossi: "No, no!" Tosca: "Listen: I can bear no more..." Cavaradossi is still strong, "Don't be silly! What do you know? What can you say?" This is one tough guy, huh? Scarpia, infuriated even more by Cavaradossi's words, shouts at Spoletta, "Make him quiet!"

Tosca: "What harm have I done to you?" She's speaking to Scarpia, of course. "It is I whom you are torturing. You are torturing my soul...Yes, it is my soul you are torturing!" This scene has gotten so ugly, my friends, and so rude, with Tosca looking at the torturing and Cavaradossi screaming and Scarpia saying, "Make him quiet," that even Spoletta, who is one of Scarpia's henchmen, mutters a prayer. That's how nasty this is. When the bad guys start getting upset, you know that a lot of ugliness is transpiring.

Scarpia goes to the torture chamber and signals for the torture to recommence. Cavaradossi's voice, "Ahhhhhh!" Tosca, at Cavaradossi's cry, she leaps up and in a stifled voice hurriedly says to Scarpia, "In the well...in the garden..." "Angelotti is there?" "Yes..."

Scarpia: *"Basta, Roberti."* "Enough, Roberti." Sciarrone, appearing at the door, "He has fainted!" Tosca, to Scarpia, "Murderer!...I want to see him..." So Scarpia says, "Carry him in."

I'm just sweating reading this stuff and I'm not even sitting in the torture chamber myself. Charles Osborne writes of this scene, and now I quote:

> Slowly and inexorably the brutality emerges. It is this scene which is both the most effective and the most sickening in *Tosca* as Puccini piles on the agony. Cavaradossi's offstage cries of pain, the nerve-grating orchestral phrases, which

depict the application of physical torture, Scarpia's cat-and-mouse manner with Tosca, her shrieks of desperation and despair all combine to increase the tension until, until Tosca confesses that she can bear no more and reveals Angelotti's whereabouts to Scarpia.

Let's listen to this and as we listen, ask yourselves what other opera or opera composers we have studied thus far could or would write such a scene? Monteverdi's *Orfeo*, everything so highly stylized and abstracted? Never. Opera seria? Grand characters, but grand characters being grand. A torturer would imply evil but never actually conduct it onstage. Opera buffa? No. I can think of no torture scenes offhand in opera buffa. In fact, even as we move through the dramatic operas of the nineteenth century, one cannot come up with a scene like this, not even in Wagner. No, no, no, no. This is verismo; this is the true depiction of the ugly side, the downside, the desperate side of desperate human beings; and Scarpia is a desperately, dastardly human being. We see it, we hear it, we feel it. We are witness to it.

Torture scene, Part Two. (musical example)

Now Tosca and Mario, a tad bit worse for the wear we might add, are reunited. Cavaradossi is carried in, unconscious, by the police-agents who lay him down on the settee. Tosca runs to him, but so great is her horror at the sight of her lover, streaming with blood, that she covers her face so as not to see him. Then, ashamed of her weakness, she kneels down beside him, kissing him and weeping.

During the course of the following dialogue, which I will not read, Tosca admits to Cavaradossi that she has ratted Angelotti out. And Cavaradossi, who has gone through a bit of stress in the last few minutes himself, is, of course, infuriated.

He screams at Tosca as he comes to, "Curses on you!" but with great timing—it is opera after all—Sciarrone, one of the henchmen, runs in, much agitated. "Excellency, terrible news!" A very good time for a change of subject.

Scarpia: "Why this long face?" Sciarrone: "News of a defeat!" Scarpia: "What defeat? How? Where?" Sciarrone: "At Marengo." Scarpia: "Idiot! You've got it wrong." Sciarrone: "Bonaparte was victorious." Scarpia says, "But, General Melas..." Sciarrone responds, "No. Melas was routed."

So Melas's victory is not a victory after all. The forces of France, the forces of liberation have been victorious and they will undoubtedly soon march on Rome.

Cavaradossi lives. He's heard all of this with growing anxiety. In his enthusiasm he finds the strength to rise and he confronts Scarpia. Cavaradossi screams out and I would tell you on a high A, but a sustained high A, that's getting—A-sharp, excuse me, even higher than an A, an A-sharp—this is very close to the top of the tenor's range and if a tenor's got a voice that can pull this off, they've got a voice. I would imagine more than one tenor has crashed and burned on "*Vittoria! Vittoria!*" on a high A-sharp.

Cavaradossi continues to sing, "Let the dawn of vengeance appear to strike terror into our foes! Let freedom arise and tyrants be overthrown!" Tosca, meanwhile, has a more pragmatic view of all of this, like, "Mario, shut up, please." She holds onto him and tries to calm him down. She says, "Hush, Mario, for my sake!"

Cavaradossi will not be refused, "You shall see me rejoice," he says to Scarpia, "for the anguish I have suffered...Let your heart falter, O Scarpia, you butcher!" Scarpia's not terribly impressed right now. After all, he still has his police and Mario is still his prisoner. Scarpia says, "Bluster and bawl! Hasten to reveal to me the depths of your infamous soul! Go! The gallows awaits you, half dead as you already are." He shouts to the police, "Take him out of here!"

Sciarrone and the police-agents seize Cavaradossi and they drag him toward the door. Tosca tries to oppose them with all of her might, clinging onto Mario as he's dragged across the room. Tosca is, of course, crying, "Ah...Mario, Mario...I will go with you..." Scarpia, pushing her back into the room, says, "Not you!"

Let's listen to this extraordinary scene, this proclamation of victory on that high A-sharp by Mario Cavaradossi and the realization that his fate would seem to be sealed. The only people left in this room after this, again, extraordinary and seemingly climactic scene, are Scarpia and Tosca. One climactic moment piled upon the next.

(musical example)

It's a brilliant trio. It really is. It's short but extraordinarily dramatic, as all three players are involved, tremendous physical action going on simultaneously, very effective theater, very effective opera.

A despairing Tosca, her soul and spirit battered and indeed almost broken, begs for Cavaradossi's life. She says to Scarpia, "Save him." Scarpia: "I? No, you." He goes back to the table, sees his interrupted supper and turns his back, calm and smiling.

In Tosca's eyes it should be settled. The bottom line is, she has confessed. He knows where Angelotti is. What's this rotten creep holding out for at this point? She has not a clue, but soon she will know. Scarpia says, "My poor supper was interrupted. Why so despondent? Oh, come, lovely lady. Sit down here. Shall we together seek some way of saving him? So then be seated. We'll talk it over, meanwhile, a glass of Spanish wine? A sip will raise your spirits."

Let the negotiations begin. Tosca, facing Scarpia and looking him right in the eye, says, *"Quanto?"* "How much?" Scarpia says, "How much?" "What's your price?" It appears that there's some steel in Tosca after all. Scarpia should see this as a bad sign but he does not.

Scarpia says, and this is a wonderful aria, perhaps Scarpia's best aria in the whole opera:

> Ah! They call me venal, but I don't sell myself to lovely ladies for mere money. If I have to betray my sworn loyalty, I choose a different payment. I've been waiting for this moment. Love of the diva has long consumed me!...But a while ago I saw you as I had never seen you before! Your tears flowed like lava on my senses, and your eyes, which darted hatred at me, made my desire all the more fierce! When, supple as a leopard, you clung to your lover, ah, in that moment I swore that you should be mine!

He advances on Tosca and, of course, with stunned realization she suddenly figures out what he wants; and what he wants is her. She lets out an agonizing cry of, "Ah!"

Let's listen to this scene, the beginning of the negotiations.

(musical example)

Disgusted, repelled, Tosca realizes nevertheless, that she truly has no choice. If Mario is to live, she must trade herself for his life. I move quickly through the intervening material to her famous aria, Tosca's response to this aria of Scarpia's, and that is *"Vissi d'arte,"* "I have lived for art."

Overcome by grief, Tosca falls on the settee. Scarpia coldly continues to gaze at her and she says, *"Vissi d'arte, vissi d'amore..."*

> I have lived for art, I have lived for love, and never harmed a living soul! In secret I have given aid to as many unfortunates as I have known. Always a true believer, I have offered up my prayers at the holy shrines; always a true believer, I have laid flowers on the altar. In my hour of tribulation why, O Lord, why hast Thou repaid me thus? I gave jewels for the Madonna's mantle, and offered my singing to the starry heavens, that they might smile more brightly. In my hour of tribulation, why, O Lord, why hast Thou repaid me thus?

This is one of Puccini's most famous, and deservedly beloved arias. It is broad, lyric and very prayerful because she's not even looking at Scarpia at this point. She's praying to her God and asking simply, "Why?" Let's listen to the very opening of this aria. Frankly and sadly, it's all we have time for; then we will continue. I would point out that this is a desperately beautiful oasis in a sea of otherwise brutal music here in the second act. *"Vissi d'arte."*

(musical example)

We know, if we've seen *Tosca*, that traditionally Tosca sings *"Vissi d'arte"* from her knees, not standing and not sitting. The story behind that is most interesting. Maria Jeritza was Puccini's favorite Tosca. It was Jeritza who started the tradition of singing *"Vissi d'arte"* from the floor. She claimed in an interview that she gave in 1926 that during a rehearsal the baritone playing Scarpia accidentally pushed her off the couch, and she did not have time to get up. "Never do it any other way," shouted Puccini from the back of the auditorium. "It was from God!" And indeed, it is. It's a marvelous and dramatic moment, but it doesn't last forever; reality re-intrudes.

Scarpia says to her, "Make up your mind." Tosca says, "Must I kneel and beg for pity? Look, I implore you with clasped hands. See, here I am defeated, pleading for a single word of mercy." Scarpia responds, "Tosca, you are too lovely and too enchanting. I yield. The bargain is a poor one. You asked for a life; I ask of you for but a moment. Well then?" Tosca nods her head in assent. Then, weeping for shame, she buries her head in the cushions of the settee.

Tosca says, "But I want him set free at once." Scarpia says, "A deception will be necessary. I cannot simply let him go. Everyone must believe that the cavalier is dead." He points to Spoletta, "This worthy fellow will arrange it." Tosca: "What assurance have I?" Scarpia says, "The order I shall give him in your presence. Spoletta, shut the door."

Then he says to Spoletta, Scarpia does, "I've changed my mind, that the prisoner will be shot, pay attention, just as we did with Count Palmieri." Scarpia gazes meaningfully at Spoletta, who nods his head to indicate he has understood Scarpia's intentions. "A firing squad," says Spoletta. "Yes, yes," Scarpia says. "A sham one, as in the case of Palmieri. Is it properly understood?" Spoletta says, "Yes, yes, just like Palmieri," wink, wink, wink, wink, wink.

Does Tosca really suspect nothing at this moment? Is she simply too exhausted to notice the subterfuge? Is she willing to believe anything at this point or is she simply not particularly bright? You take your pick, but I think she has simply been worn down and hears only what she wants to hear; she sees only what she's willing to see. Clearly, Scarpia has no intention of allowing Mario to live. In any case, Scarpia says to her, "I have kept my promise…"

Now, the final scene of Act Two, the death of Scarpia.

Tosca: "Not yet. I want a safe-conduct so that I can flee the state with him." Scarpia says, "You want to leave?" Tosca says, "Yes, for good!" Scarpia says, "You shall have your way." At that moment we hear a tragic, almost ominous theme, which portends the brutality to come. (piano example) He goes to a desk and begins to write, breaking off to ask Tosca, "Which road will you take?" Tosca says, "The shortest." "Civitavecchia?" Tosca responds, "Sì."

While Scarpia is writing, Tosca approaches the table and with trembling hand, takes the glass of Spanish wine that he poured for her earlier; but as she raises the glass to her lips she perceives on the table a sharp-pointed knife. Yes, yes! This is Scarpia's dinner knife. This is where he was eating his dinner. She casts a rapid glance at Scarpia who at that moment is busy writing, and with infinite caution succeeds in taking possession of the knife. She hides it behind her, leaning on the table and watching Scarpia. Having finished writing the safe-conduct and put his seal on it, he folds the paper; then opening his arms, he advances on Tosca to embrace her.

Scarpia says, "Tosca, at last you are mine!" But his tone changes from rapture to a terrible, painful cry; Tosca has stabbed him in the heart. "A curse on you!" Tosca: "That was Tosca's kiss!" Scarpia, staggering, tries to clutch at Tosca, who recoils in terror. Scarpia yells, "Help!…I'm dying!…Help!…I'm dying!…"

Tosca is spitting words at him, "Is your blood choking you? Ah! Slain by a woman!…You tortured me so! Can you still hear? Speak! Look at me! This is Tosca, O Scarpia!" He falls to the floor, "Help!…Help!" Tosca, "Are you choking on your blood? Die you fiend! Die! Die!! Die!…He is dead!…Now I forgive him…" Tosca's hysterical rage, finally unbottled and freely expressed, borders on sadism. Listen, her reaction to Scarpia's death is almost more disturbing than Scarpia's own actions. We expected that from Scarpia, but we didn't expect this from Tosca. We understand it in retrospect, but we didn't expect it. It's a shock and it's quite terrifying.

Then, the pantomime. Without taking her eyes off Scarpia's body, she goes to the table, takes a bottle of water, dipping a napkin in it, washes the blood off her hands. Then she rearranges her hair in front of the mirror. Remembering the safe-conduct, she looks for it on the desk but can't find it. She searches elsewhere and finally sees it clutched in Scarpia's already stiffening hand. She lifts his arm then lets it fall inert after having taken the safe-conduct, which she hides in her bosom. She utters her last words, "And all Rome used to tremble before him!"

On the point of leaving, she changes her mind; she goes and takes two candles from the wall-bracket and puts them on either side of Scarpia's head. She looks around again and sees a crucifix, takes it from the wall and, carrying it reverently, kneels down and places it on Scarpia's breast. She rises and very cautiously goes out, closing the door quietly behind her. End, Act Two.

Let us go back and listen to the death of Scarpia from the moment where he says, "I have kept my promise."

(musical example)

Puccini died in 1924, leaving his last opera, *Turandot*, incomplete. *Turandot*, which we discussed way back in Lecture One, is the last of the great, grand operas. Like them or hate them, respect them or disrespect them, Puccini's operas exhibit a wonderful balance of words and music. His stories are dramatically compelling and his music heightens and deepens the dramatic meaning and expressive content of these stories. The great American soprano, Rosa Ponselle, who worked with Puccini said, "With Puccini, it's always drama, drama, drama." Words distilled, intensified, magnified by music, the whole always greater than the parts.

We reserve the final word for Richard Strauss's last opera, *Capriccio* of 1942. *Capriccio* takes place in a chateau outside of Paris about 1775, just at the time that Gluck's operatic reforms were stirring a storm of debate in Paris. *Capriccio* is an opera about opera, in particular the relationship between words and music. In a particularly delightful scene, a poet named Olivier and a composer named Flamand and a theatric director named La Roche argue the relative merits of their respective arts.

The poet says, "Music…" And this is in an opera. I love the idea of an opera about an opera, everyone arguing about the relative merits of words and music. The poet says, "Music and dance are the slaves of rhythm, they have served it since the beginning of time." The composer says, "There is more constraint in the restrictions of verse." The poet responds, "Freedom of ideas is given to poets. Who sees any boundary between content and form?" The composer responds, "Music is in every respect more full of meaning, it ascends in spheres which you cannot invade with the mind." Olivier (the poet) responds, "Not in musical abstraction but in the clearest language can I express what I'm thinking. This is what your music can never achieve." The composer responds, "My ideas exist as melodies, and what they mean to me is inexpressible. A single chord you can feel the whole world in."

The director, La Roche, says, "Ah. They are fighting each other; each claims to be more important in his art. I could spare them the trouble! In my realm they are nothing but servants." Again the poet puts up a fight, "The poet's idea is the mirror of life. All the arts must call poetry their mother!" The composer responds, "But music is the root from which everything springs. And Nature's voices sing all other arts to sleep…" The poet says, "The language of mankind alone is the soil where art can be nourished." The composer points out, "The cry of pain preceded all speech!"

Yes indeed, their debate goes on and on and on, with the realization that what they're arguing about is opera. Is it words or music? Which is transcendent? Finally the poet points out, "The composer and poet, dreadfully hampered each by the other, are wasting unspeakable labor in giving birth to opera and acting as its midwives." The count, who is present, says, "Every opera is in itself absurd..."

Let's just sample 30 seconds or so of this wonderful scene so that you can hear what this dialogue from 1942 sounds like; then let's draw some conclusions.

(musical example)

It's a wonderful scene. It's a fascinating opera, and it is the endless argument when one comes to talk about the essence of opera—is it words, is it music, or is it something greater than both? From a purely realistic, pragmatic point of view, opera is indeed an absurd thing; but as I believe we've experienced during this course, this strange and wonderful combination of words and music, with composer, ultimately the dramatist, delivers an emotional charge perhaps unique in all of the arts.

My friends, go to operas, buy recordings; and whatever you do, read the libretto and think about the story, the words; and then, and then kick back and let the music, the singing, and the sheer magical beauty of the human voice intensify the word and transport you to a frankly heightened reality, a reality that words alone cannot create. Be it Italian, French, German, Russian, English, Czech or Spanish, be it Baroque or buffa, Wagner or Verdi, opera is an experience, a joy like no other. I wish you the very best of listening. Thank you.

Die Zauberflöte

The Magic Flute (1791)

Wolfgang Amadeus Mozart

Libretto by Emanuel Schikaneder

Tamino	**Tamino**
(regains consciousness, looks around, frightened)	*(regains consciousness, looks around, frightened)*
Wo bin ich?	Where am I?
Ist's Phantasie, dass ich noch lebe?	Is it fantasy that I am still alive?
(rises and looks around)	*(rises and looks around)*
Die Schlange tot?	That awful snake dead at my feet?
(The sound of a panpipe is heard.)	*(The sound of a panpipe is heard.)*
Was hör ich?	What do I hear?

(Withdraws, observing. Papageno, dressed in a suit of feathers, hurries by, carrying a large birdcage on his back and a panpipe in his hands.)

NO. 2 ARIA

Papageno	**Papageno**
A	*A*
Der Vogelfänger bin ich ja,	I am a man of widespread fame,
stets lustig, heissa, hopsassa!	and Papageno is my name.
Ich Vogelfänger bin bekannt	To tell you all in simple words:
bei alt und jung im ganzen Land.	I make my living catching birds.
Weiss mit dem Locken umzugehn	The moment they attract my eye
und mich aufs Pfeifen zu verstehn.	I spread my net and in they fly.
Drum kann ich froh und lustig sein,	I whistle on my pipe of Pan.
denn alle Vögel sind ja mein.	In short, I am a happy man.
(He whistles and then removes the cage from his back.)	*(He whistles and then removes the cage from his back.)*
A'	*A'*
Der Vogelfänger bin ich ja,	Although I am a happy man,
stets lustig, heissa, hopsassa!	I also have a future plan.
Ich Vogelfänger bin bekannt	I dearly love my feathered friends,
bei alt und jung im ganzen Land.	but that's not where my int'rest ends.
Ein Netz für Mädchen möchte ich,	To tell the truth, I'd like to find
ich fing sie dutzendweis für mich;	a pretty girl of my own kind.
dann sperrte ich sie bei mir ein,	In fact, I'd like to fill my net
und alle Mädchen wären mein.	with all the pretty girls I met.

Wenn alle Mädchen wären mein,
so tauschte ich brav Zucker ein;
Die, welche mir am liebsten wär,
der gäb ich gleich den Zucker her,
und küsste sie mich zärtlich dann,
wär sie mein Weib und ich ihr Mann.
Sie schlief an meiner Seite ein,
ich wiegte wie ein Kind sie ein.
(He whistles and turns to leave.)

Tamino

(steps in his way)
He da!

Papageno

Was da?

Tamino

Sag' mir, du lustiger Freund, wer bist
du?

Papageno

Wer ich bin?
(to himself)
Dumme Frage!
(to Tamino)
Ein Mensch wie du!

Once all the girls were in my net
I'd keep the fairest for my pet,
my sweetheart and my bride-to-be,
to love and cherish tenderly.
I'd bring her cake and sugar plums,
and be content to eat the crumbs.
She'd share my little nest with me —
a happier pair could never be!
(He whistles and turns to leave.)

Tamino

(steps in his way)
Hey there!

Papageno

Who's there?

Tamino

Tell me who you are, my jolly
friend.

Papageno

Who I am?
(to himself)
Silly question!
(to Tamino)
A man, like you.

Der Freischütz

The Magic Bullets (1821)

Carl Maria von Weber

Libretto by Johann Friedrich Kind

Wolf's Glen Scene

A frightful glen with a waterfall. A pallid full moon. A storm is brewing. In
the foreground a withered tree shattered by lightning seems to glow. In other
trees, owls, ravens, and other wild birds. Caspar, without a hat or coat, but
with hunting pouch and knife, is laying out a circle of black fieldstones, in
the center of which lies a skull. A few steps away a hacked-off eagle wing, a
ladle, and bullet moulds.

Chorus of Invisible Spirits

Milch des Mondes fiel auf's Kraut
Uhui! Uhui!
Spinnweb' ist mit Blut bethaut!
Eh' noch wieder Abend graut,
Uhui! Uhui!
Ist sie todt, die zarte Braut!
Eh' noch wieder sinkt die Nacht,
ist das Opfer dargebracht!
*(A clock in the distance strikes twelve.
The circle of stones is completed.)*

Caspar

Samiel! Samiel! erschein!
Bei des Zaub'rers Hirngebein!
Samiel! Samiel! erschein!

Samiel

(steps out of a rock)
Was rufst du mich?

Caspar

(throws himself at Samiel's feet)
Du weisst, dass meine Frist
Schier abgelaufen ist.

Chorus of Invisible Spirits

The milk of the moon fell on the
herbs. Uhui! Uhui!
Spiderwebs dabbed with blood.
Before another evening darkens,
Uhui! Uhui!
will she die, the lovely bride.
Before another night falls,
will the sacrifice be offered.
*(A clock in the distance strikes twelve.
The circle of stones is completed.)*

Caspar

Samiel! Samiel! appear!
By the wizard's skull-bone,
Samiel! Samiel! appear!

Samiel

(steps out of a rock)
Why do you call me?

Caspar

(throws himself at Samiel's feet)
You know that my days of grace
are coming to an end.

Samiel

Morgen!

Caspar

Verläng're sie noch einmal mir!

Samiel

No!

Caspar

Ich bringe neue Opfer dir.

Samiel

Welche?

Caspar

Mein Jagdgesell,
er naht, er, der
noch nie dein dunkles Reich betrat.

Samiel

Was sein Begehr?

Caspar

Freikugeln sind's, auf die er
Hoffnung baut.

Samiel

Sechse treffen, seiben äffen!

Caspar

Die siebente sei dein!
Aus seinem Rohr lenk' sie nach
seiner Braut!
Dies wird ihn der Verzweiflung
weih'n, ihn, und den Vater.

Samiel

Noch hab' ich keinen Teil an ihr.

Samiel

Tomorrow!

Caspar

Will you extend them once more?

Samiel

No!

Caspar

I bring you new sacrifices.

Samiel

Which ones?

Caspar

My hunting companion,
he approaches, who has never before
set foot in your dark kingdom.

Samiel

What does he want?

Caspar

Magic bullets, in which he puts his
hope.

Samiel

Six strike, seven deceive!

Caspar

The seventh is yours!
From his own gun it will aim at his
bride.
That will drive him to despair,
both he and his father.

Samiel

I side with neither party.

Caspar

(afraid)

Genügt er dir allein?

Samiel

Das findet sich!

Caspar

Doch schenkst du Frist,
und wieder auf drei Jahr,
bring ich ihn dir zu Beute dar!

Samiel

Es sei! Bei den Pforten der Hölle!
Morgen, Er oder Du!

(He disappears amidst thunder. Also the skull and knife disappear. In their place a small stove with glowing coals is seen.)

———□———

Caspar

(He takes the ingredients from his pouch and throws them in one by one.)
Hier erst das Blei. Ewas gestossenes
Glas von zerbrochenen
Kirchenfenstern,
das findet sich. Etwas Quecksilber.
Drei Kugeln, die schon einmal
getroffen. Das rechte Auge eines
Wiedehopfs, das linke eines Luchses.
Probatum est! Und nun den
Kugelsegen!

———□———

Caspar

(afraid)

Will he be sufficient for you?

Samiel

Perhaps.

Caspar

If you will grant me grace
for another three years,
I will bring him to you as prey.

Samiel

So be it. By the gates of hell,
Tomorrow: he or you!

Caspar

(He takes the ingredients from his pouch and throws them in one by one.)
First, then, the lead. Then this
piece of glass from a
broken church
window, some mercury,
three balls that have already hit the
mark. The right eye of a
lapwing, and the left of a lynx.
Probatum est! Now to bless the
bullets.

Melodrama

Caspar

(pausing three times, bowing to the earth)

Schütze, der im Dunkel wacht.
Samiel! Samiel! Hab' acht!
Steh mir bei in dieser Nacht,
Bis der Zauber is vollbracht!
Salbe mir so Kraut als Blei,
Segn' es sieben, neun und drei,
Dass die Kugel tüchtig sei!
Samiel! Samiel! Herbei!

Caspar

(pausing three times, bowing to the earth)

Hunter, who watches in the darkness,
Samiel! Samiel! Pay attention!
Stay with me through this night
until the magic is achieved.
Anoint for me the herbs and lead.
Bless the seven, nine and three,
so that the bullet will be fit.
Samiel! Samiel! Come to me!

(The material in the crucible begins to hiss and bubble, sending forth a greenish flame. A cloud passes over the moon, obscuring the light. He casts the first bullet, which drops in the pan.)

EINS!   ONE!

(The echo repeats: EINS! Nightbirds crowd around the fire.)

ZWEI!   TWO!

(The echo repeats: ZWEI! A black boar passes. Startled, he counts.)

DREI!   THREE!

(Echo: DREI! A storm starts to rage. He continues to count anxiously.)

VIER!   FOUR!

(Echo: VIER! Cracking of whips and the sound of galloping horses is heard. Caspar is more and more alarmed.)

FÜNF!   FIVE!

(Echo: FÜNF! Dogs barking and horses neighing are heard: the devil's hunt.)

Wehe! Das wilde Heer!   Woe is me! The wild chase!

Chorus

Durch Berg und Thal,
durch Schlucht und Schacht,
durch Thau und Wolken,
Sturm und Nacht!
Durch Höhle, Sumpf und Erdenkluft,

Chorus

Through hill and dale,
through glen and mire,
through dew and night!
storm and night!
Through marsh, swamp and chasm,

durch Feuer, Erde, See und Luft, Jo ho! Wau wau! Jo ho! Wau wau! Ho ho ho ho ho ho ho ho!	through fire, earth, sea and air, Yo ho! Wow wow! Jo ho! Wow wow! Ho ho ho ho ho ho ho ho!

Caspar | **Caspar**

SECHS! | SIX!

(Echo: SECHS! Deepest darkness. The storm lashes with terrific force.)

Samiel! Samiel! Samiel! Hilf! *(Samiel appears.)*	Samiel! Samiel! Samiel! Help! *(Samiel appears.)*

Samiel | **Samiel**

Hier bin ich! *(Caspar is hurled to the ground)*	Here I am. *(Caspar is hurled to the ground.)*

Max | **Max**

(nearly losing his balance from the impact of the storm; he jumps out of the magic circle and grips a dead branch, shouting)

Samiel! | Samiel!

(The storm suddenly dies down. Instead of the dead tree, the black hunter appears before Max, grabbing his hand.)

Samiel | **Samiel**

Hier bin ich! | Here I am.

(Max makes the sign of the cross as he is thrown to the ground. The clock strikes one. Dead silence. Samiel has disappeared. Caspar remains motionless, face to the ground. Max rises convulsively.)

———□———

Tristan und Isolde

(1859)

Richard Wagner

Libretto by the composer

ACT ONE

Scene Five

Sailors

(outside)
Auf das Tau!
Anker ab!

Tristan

(starting wildly)
Los den Anker!
Das Steuer dem Strom!
Den Winden Segel und Mast!
(He takes the cup from Isolde)
Wohl kenn' ich Irlands Königin,
und ihrer Künste Wunderkraft:
den Balsam nütz' ich, den sie bot:
den Becher nehm' ich nun,
dass ganz ich heut' genese.
Und achte auch des Sünne eid's,
den ich zum Dank dir sage.
Tristans Ehre, höchste Treu!
Tristans Elend, kühnster Trotz!
Trug des Herzens!
Traum der Ahnung:
ew'ger Trauer einz'ger Trost:
Vergessens güt'ger Trank,
dich trink' ich sonder Wank.
(He sits and drinks)

Isolde

Betrug auch hier?
Mein die Hälfte!

Sailors

(outside)
Haul the line.
Drop the anchor.

Tristan

(starting wildly)
Drop the anchor!
Stern to the current!
Sail and mast to the wind!
(He takes the cup from Isolde)
Well know I Ireland's Queen,
and her art's magic.
The balsam I used that she brought.
The goblet I now take so that
I might altogether today recover.
And heed also the oath of atonement,
which I thankfully made to you.
Tristan's honor, highest truth!
Tristan's anguish, brave defiance!
Betrayal of the heart!
Dream of presentiment,
eternal sorrow, unique solace,
forgetting's kindly draught,
I drink without wavering.
(He sits and drinks)

Isolde

Betrayed even in this?
The half is mine!

(She wrests the cup from his hand)
Verräter! Ich trink' sie dir!
(She drinks, and then throws away the cup. Both, seized with shuddering, gaze at each other with deepest agitation, still with stiff demeanor, as the expression of defiance of death fades into a glow of passion. Trembling grips them. They convulsively clutch their hearts and pass their hands over their brows. Then they seek each other with their eyes, sink into confusion, and once more turn with renewed longing toward each other.)

Isolde

(with wavering voice)
Tristan!

Tristan

(overwhelmed)
Isolde!

Isolde

(sinking on his chest)
Treuloser Holder!

Tristan

Seligste Frau!
(He embraces her with ardor. They remain in silent embrace.)

All the Men

(outside)
Heil! Heil!
König Marke!
König Marke, Heil!

Brangäne

(who, with averted face, full of confusion and horror, had leaned over the side, turns to see the pair sunk into a love embrace, and hurls herself, wringing her hands, into the foreground)
Wehe! Weh!
Unabwendbar ew'ge Not
für kurzen Tod!

(She wrests the cup from his hand)
Traitor, I drink to you!

Isolde

(with wavering voice)
Tristan!

Tristan

(overwhelmed)
Isolde!

Isolde

(sinking on his chest)
Treacherous lover!

Tristan

Divine woman!
(He embraces her with ardor. They remain in silent embrace.)

All the Men

(outside)
Hail! Hail!
King Mark!
King Mark, Hail!

Brangäne

Woe's me! Woe's me!
Inevitable, endless distress,
instead of quick death!

Tör'ger Treue trugvolles Werk
Blüht nun jammernd empor!
(*They break from their embrace.*)

Misleading truth, deceitful work
now blossoms pitifully upward.
(*They break from their embrace.*)

Tristan

(*bewildered*)
Was träumte mir
von Tristans Ehre?

Tristan

(*bewildered*)
What did I dream
of Tristan's honor?

Isolde

Was träumte mir
von Isoldes Schmach?

Isolde

What did I dream
of Isolde's disgrace?

Tristan

Du mir verloren?

Tristan

Are you lost to me?

Isolde

Du mich verstossen?

Isolde

Have you repulsed me?

Tristan

Trügenden Zaubers Tückische List!

Tristan

False magic's nasty trick!

Isolde

Törigen Zürnes Eitles Dräu'n!

Isolde

Foolish wrath's vain menace!

Tristan

Isolde! Süsseste Maid!

Tristan

Isolde, Sweetest maiden!

Isolde

Tristan! Trautester Mann!

Isolde

Tristan; most beloved man!

Both

Wie sich die Herzen wogend
erheben,
wie alle Sinne wonnig erbeben!
Sehnender Minne
schwellendes Blühen,
schmachtender Liebe seliges Glühen!
Jach in der Brust
jauchzende Lust!

Both

How, heaving, our hearts are
uplifted!
How all our senses blissfully quiver!
Longing, passion,
swelling blooms,
languishing love, blessed glow!
Precipitate in the breast
exulting desire!

Isolde! Tristan!
Tristan! Isolde!
Welten entronnen
du mir gewonnen!
Du mir einzig bewusst,
höchste Liebeslust!

Isolde! Tristan!
Tristan! Isolde!
Escaped from the world,
you have won me.
You, my only thought,
highest love's desire!

(The curtains are now drawn wide apart. The entire ship is filled with knights and sailors, who joyfully signal the shore from aboard. Nearby is seen a cliff crowned by a castle. Tristan and Isolde remain lost in mutual contemplation, unaware of what is taking place.)

Brangäne

(to the women, who at her bidding ascend from below)
Schnell den Mantel,
den Königsschmuck!
(rushing between Tristan and Isolde)
Unsel'ge! Auf!
Hört, wo wir sind.
(She puts the royal cloak on Isolde, who does not notice anything.)

Brangäne

(to the women, who at her bidding ascend from below)
Quick, the cloak,
the royal robe.
(rushing between Tristan and Isolde)
Up, unfortunate pair! Up!
See where we are!
(She puts the royal cloak on Isolde, who does not notice anything.)

All the Men

Heil! Heil!
König Marke!
König Marke, Heil!

All the Men

Hail, hail!
King Mark!
King Mark, hail!

Kurwenal

(advancing cheerfully)
Heil Tristan!
glücklicher Held!
Mit reichem Hofgesinde
dort auf Nachen Naht Herr Marke.
Heil! wie die Fahrt ihn freut,
dass er die Braut sich freit!

Kurwenal

(advancing cheerfully)
Hail, Tristan!
Fortunate hero!
With splendid courtiers
there in the skiff Mark approaches.
Ah, how the ride delights him,
for soon he will be wooing the bride.

Tristan

(looking up, bewildered)
Wer naht?

Tristan

(looking up, bewildered)
Who comes?

Kurwenal

Der König!

Tristan

Welcher König?
(*Kurwenal points over the side.
Tristan stares stupefied at the shore.*)

All the Men

(*waving their hats*)
Heil! König Marke!

Isolde

(*confused*)
Marke! Was will er?
Was ist, Brangäne!
Welcher Ruf?

Brangäne

Isolde! Herrin! Fassung nur heut!

Isolde

Wo bin ich? Leb' ich?
Ha! Welcher Trank?

Brangäne

(*despairingly*)
Der Liebestrank!

Isolde

(*stares, frightened, at Tristan*)
Tristan!

Tristan

Isolde!

Isolde

(*She falls, fainting, upon his chest.*)
Muss ich leben?

Kurwenal

The King.

Tristan

Which King?
(*Kurwenal points over the side.
Tristan stares stupefied at the shore.*)

All the Men

(*waving their hats*)
Hail, King Mark!

Isolde

(*confused*)
Mark! What does he want?
What is that, Brangäne?
What is the shouting?

Brangäne

Isolde! Mistress, get hold of yourself.

Isolde

Where am I? Am I alive?
Oh, what drink was it?

Brangäne

(*despairingly*)
The love potion.

Isolde

(*stares, frightened, at Tristan*)
Tristan!

Tristan

Isolde!

Isolde

(*She falls, fainting, upon his chest.*)
Must I live?

Brangäne

(to the women)
Helft der Herrin!

Tristan

O Wonne voller Tücke!
O Truggeweihtes Glücke!

All the Men

(in a general acclamation)
Heil dem König Kornwall, Heil!
(People have climbed over the ship's side, others have extended a bridge, and the atmosphere is one of expectation of the arrival of those that have been awaited, as the curtain falls.)

Brangäne

(to the women)
Help your mistress!

Tristan

O rapture full of cunning!
O fraudulently won good fortune!

All the Men

(in a general acclamation)
Hail the King! Hail, Cornwall!

ACT THREE

Scene Three

Isolde

(unconscious of all around her, turning her eyes on Tristan's body with rising inspiration)
Mild und leise wie er lächelt,
wie das Auge hold er öffnet—
seht ihr's, Freunde? Seht ihr's nicht?
Immer lichter wie er leuchtet,
stern-umstrahlet hoch sich hebt?
Seht ihr's nicht?
Wie das Herz ihm mutig schwillt,
voll und hehr im Busen ihm quillt?
Wie den Lippen, wonnig mild,
süßer Atem sanft entweht—
Freunde! Seht!
Fühlt und seht ihr's nicht?
Hör' ich nur diese Weise,
die so wundervoll und leise,
Wonne klagend, alles sagend,

Isolde

(unconscious of all around her, turning her eyes on Tristan's body with rising inspiration)
See him smiling, softly, gently,
see the eyes that open fondly,
O my friends here, don't you see?
Ever lighter how he's shining,
borne on high amid the stars?
Don't you see?
How his heart so bravely swells,
full and calm it throbs in his breast!
How from lips so joyful-mild
sweet the breath that softly stirs—
Friends! See!
Don't you feel and see?
Is it only I who hear these
gentle, wondrous strains of music,
joyously sounding, telling all things,

mild versöhnend aus ihm tönend,	reconciling, sounding from him,
in mich dringet, auf sich schwinget,	piercing through me, rising upward,
hold erhallend um mich klinget?	echoes fondly round me ringing?
Heller schallend, mich umwallend,	Ever clearer, wafting round me,
sind es Wellen sanfter Lüfte?	are they waves or gentle breezes?
Sind es Wogen	Are they clouds of
wonniger Düfte?	gladdening perfumes?
Wie sie schwellen, mich umrauschen,	As they swell and murmur round me,
soll ich atmen, soll ich lauschen?	shall I breathe them, shall I listen?
Soll ich schlürfen, untertauchen?	Shall I sip them, plunge beneath them,
Süß in Düften mich verhauchen?	breathe my last amid their fragrance?
In dem wogenden Schwall,	In the billowy surge,
in dem tönenden Schall,	in the ocean of sound,
in des Welt-Atems wehendem All,	in the World Spirit's infinite All,
ertrinken, versinken—	to drown now, descending,
unbewußt—höchste Lust!	void of thought—highest bliss!

(Isolde sinks, as if transfigured, in Brangäne's arms upon Tristan's body. Profound emotion and grief of the bystanders. Mark invokes a blessing on the dead.)

—▢—

Salome

(1905)

Richard Strauss

Libretto by Hedwig Lachmann

Narraboth

Die Prinzessin erhebt sich! Sie verlässt die Tafel. Sie ist sehr erregt. Sie kommt hierher.

Page der Herodias

Sieh sie nicht an!

Narraboth

Ja, sie kommt auf uns zu.

Page der Herodias

Ich bitte dich, sieh sie nicht an!

Narraboth

Sie ist wie eine verirrte Taube.

Narraboth

The Princess rises! She is leaving the table! She looks very troubled. She is coming this way.

Page of Herodias

Do not look at her.

Narraboth

Yes, she is coming towards us.

Page of Herodias

I pray you not to look at her.

Narraboth

She is like a dove that has strayed.

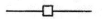

(Salome enters, very excited.)

Salome

Ich will nicht blieben. Ich kann nicht bleiben. Warum sieht mich der Tetrarch fortwährend so an mit seinen Maulwurfsaugen unter den zuckenden Lidern? Es ist seltsam, dass der Mann meiner Mutter mich so ansieht.
Wie süss ist hier die Luft. Hier kann ich atmen. Da drinnen sitzen Juden aus Jerusalem, die einander über ihre närrischen Gebräuche in Stücke reissen.

(Salome enters, very excited.)

Salome

I will not stay. I cannot stay. Why does the Tetrarch look at me all the while with his mole's eyes under his shaking eyelids? It is strange that the husband of my mother looks at me like that.
How sweet the air is here. I can breathe here. Within there are Jews from Jerusalem who are tearing each other in pieces over their foolish ceremonies.

Schweigsame, listge Egypter und brutale, ungeschlachte Römer mit ihrer plumpen Sprache. O, wie ich diese Römer hasse!

Silent subtle Egyptians and brutal, coarse Romans with their uncouth jargon. Ah, how I loathe the Romans!

Page der Herodias

Schreckliches wird geschehn. Warum siehst du sie so an?

Page of Herodias

Something terrible will happen. Why do you look at her?

Salome

Wie gut ist's, in den Mond zu sehn. Er ist wie eine silberne Blume, kühl und keusch. Ja, wie die Schönheit einer Jungfrau, die rein geblieben ist.

Salome

How good to see the moon! She is like a silver flower, cold and chaste. Yes, I am sure she is a virgin, she has a virgin's beauty.

Stimme des Jokanaan

Siehe, der Herr is gekommen, des Menschen Sohn ist nahe.

Voice of John

The lord hath come. The son of man hath come.

Salome

Wer war das, der hier gerufen hat?

Salome

Who was that who cried out?

Zweiter Soldat

Der Prophet, Prinzessin.

Second Soldier

The prophet, Princess.

Salome

Ach, der Prophet. Der, vor dem der Tetrarch Angst hat?

Salome

Ah, the prophet! He of whom the Tetrarch is afraid?

Zweiter Soldat

Wir wissen davon nichts, Prinzessin. Es war der Prophet Jokanaan der hier rief.

Second Soldier

We know nothing of that, Princess. It was the prophet Jokanaan who cried out.

Narraboth

Beliebt es Euch, dass ich eure Sänfte holen lasse, Prinzessin? Die Nacht ist schön im Garten.

Narraboth

Is it your pleasure that I bid them bring your litter, Princess? The night is fair in the garden.

Salome

Er sagt schreckliche Dinge über
meine Mutter, nicht wahr?

Salome

He says terrible things about my
mother, does he not?

(The prophet comes out of the cistern. Salome looks at him and steps slowly back.)

Jokanaan

Wo ist er, dessen Sündenbecher jatzt
voll ist? Wo ist er, der eines Tages im
Angesicht alles Volkes in einem
Silbermantel sterben wird?
Heisst ihn herkommen, auf dass er
die Stimme Dessen höre, der in der
Wüste und in den Häusern der
Könige gekündet hat.

John

Where is he whose cup of abominations is now full? Where is he, who in
a robe of silver shall one day die in the
face of all the people? Bid him come
forth, that he may hear the voice of
him who hath cried in the waste
places and in the houses of kings.

Salome

(Rising)

Willst du mir wirklich alles geben, was
ich von dir begehre, Tetrarch?

Salome

(Rising)

Will you indeed give me whatsoever
I shall ask, Tetrarch?

Herodias

Tanze nicht, meine Tochter.

Herodias

Do not dance, my daughter.

Herodes

Alles, alles, was du von mir begehren
wirst; und wärs die Hälfte meines
Königreichs.

Herod

Everything, whatsoever you desire I
will give it you, even to the half of
my kingdom.

Salome

Du schwörst es, Tetrarch?

Salome

You swear it, Tetrarch?

Herodes

Ich schwör' es, Salome.

Herod

I swear it, Salome.

Salome

Wobei willst du das beschwören,
Tetrarch?

Salome

By what will you swear, Tetrarch?

Herodes

Bei meinem Leben, bei meiner Krone, bei meinen Göttern.

Herod

By my life, by my crown, by my gods.

Herodias

Tanze nicht, meine Tochter!

Herodias

Do not dance, my daughter.

Herodes

O Salome, Salome, tanz für mich!

Herod

O Salome, Salome, dance for me!

Salome

Du hast einen Eid geschworen, Tetrarch.

Salome

You have sworn, Tetrarch.

Herodes

Ich habe einen Eid geschworen.

Herod

I have sworn, Salome.

Herodias

Meine Tochter, tanze nicht.

Herodias

My daughter, do not dance.

Herodes

Und wär's die Hälfte meines Königreichs. Du wirst schön sein als Königin, unermesslich schön. Ah! es ist kalt hier. Es weht ein eisger Wind, und ich höre . . . warum höre ich in der Luft dieses Rauschen von Flügeln? Ah! Es ist doch so, als ob ein ungeheurer schwarzer Vogel über der Terrasse schwebte? Warum kann ich ihn nicht sehn, diesen Vogel? Dieses Rauschen ist schrecklich. Es ist ein schneidender Wind. Aber nein, er ist nicht kalt, er ist heiss. Giesst mir Wasser über die Hände, gebt mir Schnee zu essen, macht mir den Mantel los. Schnell, schnell, macht mir den Mantel los! Doch nein! Lasst ihn! Dieser Kranz drückt mich. Diese Rosen sind wie Feuer.

Herod

Even to the half of my kingdom. Thou wilt be passing fair as a queen. Ah! it is cold here. There is an icy wind, and I hear . . . wherefore do I hear in the air this beating of wings? Ah! one might fancy a huge black bird hovers over the terrace.

Why can I not see it, this bird? The beat of its wings is terrible. It is a chill wind. Nay, but it is not cold, it is hot. Pour water on my hands. Give me snow to eat. Loosen my mantle.

Quick, quick, loosen my mantle. Nay, but leave it. It is my garland of roses that hurts me. The flowers are like fire.

(He tears the wreath from his head and throws it on the table.)
Ah! Jetzt kann ich atmen.
Jetzt bin ich glücklich.
Willst du für mich tanzen, Salome?

Herodias

Ich will nicht haben, dass sie tanze!

Salome

Ich will für dich tanzen.

(Slaves bring perfumes and the seven veils and take off the sandals of Salome.)

Stimme des Jokanaan

Wer ist Der, der von Edom kommt, wer ist Der, der von Bosra kommt, dessen Kleid mit Purpur gefärbt ist, der in der Schönheit seiner Gewänder leuchtet, der mächtig in seiner Grösse wandelt, warum ist dein Kleid mit Scharlach gefleckt?

Herodias

Wir wollen hineingehn. Die Stimme dieses Menschen macht mich wahnsinnig. Ich will nicht haben, dass meine Tochter tanzt, während er immer dazwischen schreit. Ich will nicht haben, dass sie tanzt, während du sie auf solche Art ansiehst. Mit einem Wort: ich will nicht haben, dass sie tanzt.

Herodes

Steh nicht auf, mein Weib, meine Königin. Es wird dir nichts helfen, ich gehe nicht hinein, bevor sie getanzt hat. Tanze Salome, tanz für mich!

(He tears the wreath from his head and throws it on the table.)
Ah! I can breathe now.
Now I am happy.
Will you not dance for me, Salome?

Herodias

I will not have her dance.

Salome

I will dance for you.

Voice of John

Who is this cometh from Edom, who is this who cometh from Bozra, whose raiment is dyed with purple, who shineth in the beauty of his garments, who walketh mighty in his greatness? Wherefore is thy raiment stained with scarlet?

Herodias

Let us go within. The voice of that man maddens me. I will not have my daughter dance while he is continually crying out. I will not have her dance while you look at her in this fashion. In a word, I will not have her dance.

Herod

Do not rise, my wife, my queen. It will avail thee nothing. I will not go within till she hath danced. Dance, Salome, dance for me!

Herodias

Tanze nicht, meine Tochter!

Salome

Ich bin bereit, Tetrarch.

(Salome dances the dance of the seven veils.)

Herodias

Do not dance, my daughter!

Salome

I am ready, Tetrarch.

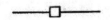

Herodes

Sie ist ein Ungeheuer, deine
Tochter. Ich sage dir, sie ist ein
Ungeheuer!

Herod

She is a monster, your daughter. I
tell you, she is a monster!

Herodias

Meine Tochter hat recht getan. Ich möchte jetzt hier bleiben.

Herodes

(Rising)

Ah! Da spricht meines Bruders Weib. Komm, ich will nicht an diesem Orte bleiben. Komm, sag ich dir! Sicher, es wird Schreckliches geschehn. Wir wollen uns im Palast verbergen, Herodias, ich fange an zu erzittern. Mannassah, Issachar, Ozias, löscht die Fackeln aus. Verbergt den Mond, verbergt die Sterne! Es wird Schreckliches geschehn.

(The slaves put out the torches. The stars disappear. A great black cloud crosses the moon and conceals it completely. The stage becomes very dark. The Tetrarch begins to climb the staircase.)

Salome

Ah! Ich habe deinen Mund geküsst, Jokanaan. Ah! Ich habe ihn geküsst, deinen Mund, es war ein bitterer Geschmack auf deinen Lippen. Hat es nach Blut geschmeckt? Nein! Doch es schmeckte vielleicht nach Liebe. . . . Sie sagen, dass die Liebe bitter schmecke. . . . Allein was tut's? Was tut's? Ich habe deinen Mund geküsst, Jokanaan. Ich habe ihn geküsst deinen Mund.

(A moonbeam falls on Salome, covering her with light.)

Herodes

(Turning round and seeing Salome.)
Man töte dieses Weib!

(The soldiers rush forward and crush beneath their shields Salome, daughter of Herodias, Princess of Judaea.)

Herodias

I approve of what my daughter has done. And I will stay here now.

Herod

(Rising)

Ah! There speaks the incestuous wife! Come! I will not stay here. Come! I tell thee. Surely some terrible thing will befall. Let us hide ourselves in our palace, Herodias, I begin to be afraid. Mannessah, Issachar, Ozias, put out the torches. Hide the moon! Hide the stars! Some terrible thing will befall.

Salome

Ah! I have kissed thy mouth, Jokanaan. Ah! I have kissed thy mouth. There was a bitter taste on thy lips. Was it the taste of blood? No! But perchance it is the taste of love. . . . They say that love hath a bitter taste. . . . But what of that? What of that? I have kissed thy mouth, Jokanaan. I have kissed thy mouth.

Herod

(Turning round and seeing Salome.)
Kill that woman!

Ruslan and Lyudmilla

(1842)

Mikhail Glinka

Libretto by Valerian Shirkov and the composer

ACT ONE

Chor	Chorus
Lel' tainstvennyj! Upoitel'nyj!	O, mysterious wonderful god of love!
Ty vostorgi l'es v serdce nam.	You pour ecstasy into our hearts;
Slavim vlast' tvoju i mogucestvo,	We glorify your power and strength,
Neizbeznye na zemle!	which cannot be avoided on earth!
Oj Dido Lado! Lel'!	O, god of love, god of love!
Ty pecal nyj mir prevrascaes' nam	You transform our sad world
V nebo	into a heaven
Radostej i utech.	of happiness and pleasure.
V noc' glubokuju,	In the depths of night,
Crez bedy i strach,	through disasters and fear,
K lozu roskosi nas vedes.	you lead us to a bed of luxury.
I volnues grud' sladostrastiem,	You fill our souls with passion
I ulybku sles' na usta.	and send a smile to our lips.
Oj Dido Lado! Lel'!	O, god of love, god of love!
No, cudesnyj Lel',	But miraculous god of love,
Ty bog revnosti:	you are also the god of jealousy,
Ty vlivaes v nas mscen'ja zar.	who pours the fever of revenge into us.
I prestupnika ty na loze neg	And on his bed of languor
Predaes vragu bez meca.	you betray the unarmed criminal to his
Tak ravnjaes' ty skorb' i radosti,	enemy. Thus you even out sorrow and
Ctoby neba nam ne zabyt'.	joy, so that we do not forget the gods.
Dido Lado! Lel'!	O, god of love!
Vse velikoe, vse prestupnoc	All that is great, all that is criminal
Smertnyj vedaet crez tebja;	mortals learn from you.
Ty za rodinu	You lead us into the terrible battle
V bitvu strasnuju,	to protect our land,
Kak na svetlyj pir nas vedes;	as if leading us to a wonderful feast.
Ucelevsemu ty venky klades'	You place a garland of laurels
Lavra vecnogo na glavu.	on the brows of the survivors,
A kto pal v boju zu otecestvo,	and you prepare a wake for those
Triznoj slavnojy usladis'!	who fell in the battle for the fatherland

Lel' tainstvennyj, usladitel'nyj,	O, mysterious wonderful god of love!
Ty vostorgi l'es' v serdce nam!	You pour ecstasy into our hearts!
(A short but loud thunderclap is heard.	*(A short but loud thunderclap is heard.*
The stage darkens.)	*The stage darkens.)*

Rondo

Farlaf

Farlaf

Blizok uz cas torzestva moego:	The hour of my triumph approaches.
Nenavistnyj sopernik ujdet daleko	My hated rival will go far away
ot nas!	from us.
Vitjaz', naprasno	O, knight, you are wasting your time
Ty isces' knjaznu,	in search of the princess.
Do nee ne dopustit volsebnicy vlast'	The witch's power will not let you get
tebja.	to her!
Ljudmila, naprasno ty places' i	Lyudmila, your tears and groans are a
stones', i milogo serdcu naprasno ty	waste of time, and you wait for your
zdes': Ni vopli, ni slezy, nicto ne	dear one in vain! Neither howls nor
pomozet! Smiris'sja pred vlast'ju	tears will do any good! Submit to
Nainy, knjazna!	Naina's power, princess!
Blizok uz cas torzestva moego, *etc.*	The hour of my triumph approaches, *etc.*
Ruslan, zabud' ty o Ljudmile!	Ruslan, forget about Lyudmila.
Ljudmila, zenicha zabud'!	Lyudmila, forget your fiancee.
Pri mysli obladat' knjaznoj	At the very thought of possessing the
Serdce radost' oscuscaet	princess my heart leaps with happiness,
I zaranee vkusaet	and I am already beginning to feel
Sladost' mesti i ljubvi.	the sweetness of revenge and love.
Blizok uz cas torzestva moego, *etc.*	The hour of my triumph approaches, *etc.*
V zabotach, v trevoge, dosade i	In travail, in anguish, annoyance, and
grusti	sadness

Skitajsja po svetu, moj chrabryj sopernik! Bejsja s vragami, vlazaj na tverdyni!	wander the world, my brave rival! Fight enemies, storm fortresses!
Ne trudjas' i ne zabotjas, Ja na namerenij dostignu, V zamke dedov ozidaja povelenija Nainy. Ne dalek zelannyj den', Den' vostorga i ljubvi!	Without working or worrying, sitting in the castle of my forefathers, awaiting the commands of Naina the desired day approaches. The day of ecstasy and love!
Ljudmila, naprasno, *etc.*	Lyudmila, your tears, *etc.*
Blizok uz cas torzestva moego, *etc.*	The hour of my triumph approaches, *etc.*
V zabotach, v trevoge, *etc.*	In travail, in anguish, *etc.*
Blizok uz cas torzestva moego, *etc.*	The hour of my triumph approaches, *etc.*

Aria

Ruslan

Ruslan

O, zizni otrada mladaja supruga! Uzel' ty ne slysis' Stenanija druga? No serdce ee trepescet i b'etsja, Ulybka porchaet Na milych ustach. Nevedomyj strach Mne dusu terzaet! O drugi! kot znaet, Ko mne li ulybka letit, I serdce po mne li drozit?	O love of my life, young wife! Can you really not hear the groans of your beloved? But her heart beats and flutters, and a smile plays on her beautiful lips. An unknown fear torments my soul! O, friends! Who knows whether her smile is for me, whether the heart beats for me?

Boris Godunov

(1874)

Modest Mussorgsky

Libretto by the composer

Bojare

Da zdravstvuet car' Boris
Feodorovic!

Narod

Da zdravstvuet!
Uz kak na nebe solncu krasnomu
Slava, slava!
Uz kak na Rusi carju Borisu
Slava, Slava, Carju Slava!
Slava! Slava! Slava! Slava!

Boris

(from the porch)
Skorbit dusa.
Kakoj-to strach nevol'nyj
Zlovescim predcuvstviem
Skoval mne serdce.
O, pravednik, o, moj
otec derzavnyj!
Vozzri s nebes na slezy
Vernych slug
I nisposli ty mne svjascennoe
Na vlast' blagoslovcn'e:
Da budu blag i praveden,
kak ty;
Da v slave pravlju svoj narod . . .
Teper' poklonimsja
Pocijuscim vlastiteljam Rossii.

(majestically)
A tam szyvat' narod na pir,
Vsech, ot bojar,

Boyars

Long live Tsar Boris
Feodorovich!

The People

Long may he live!
Like the radiant sun in the sky,
Glory, glory!
Glory, glory, glory to the Tsar,
To Boris, the Tsar of Russia!
Glory! Glory! Glory! Glory!

Boris

(from the porch)
My soul is sad.
Some sort of involuntary fear
has gripped my heart
with a sense of evil foreboding.
O, Righteous One, oh sovereign
Father of mine!
Look down from heaven on the
tears of your faithful servants
and send me a holy blessing
for my rule:
Let me be good and righteous
as you are;
may I rule my people in glory . . .
Now let us pay our respects
to the past rulers of Russia now
deceased.

(majestically)
And now invite the people to the
feast, all from boyar

Do niscego slepca,	to blind beggar,
Vsem vol'nyj vchod,	let everyone enter,
Vse, gosti dorogie!	you are all welcome!

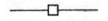

Vaarlam's Song

Vaarlam	Vaarlam
Kak vo gorode bylo,	Here's what happened at the
vo Kazani,	town of Kazan,
Groznyj car' piroval,	Ivan the Terrible was feasting
Da veselilsja.	and making merry.
On tatarej bil	He had given the Tatars
nescadno,	a ruthless beating
Ctob im bylo da ne povadno	to teach them a lesson not to
Vdol' po Rusi guljat'.	go wandering over Russia again.
Car' podchodom podchodil	The Tsar came close,
Da pod Kazan' gorodok;	to the little town of Kazan.
On podkopy podkopal,	He dug some trenches
Da, pod Kazanku reku.	under the river of Kazan.
Kak tatare-to po gorodu pochazivajut,	As the Tatars strolled about town
Na carja Ivana-to pogljadyvajut,	they stole glances at Tsar Ivan,
Zli tatarove!	those evil Tatars!
Groznyj car' ot zakrucinilsja,	Ivan the Terrible became sad,
On povesil golovusku	he hung his head
Na pravoe pleco.	on his right shoulder.
Uz kak stal car' puskarej szyvat',	The Tsar sent for the gunners,
Puskarej vse zazigal'scikov,	the gunners with all their guns,
Zazigal'scikov!	the gunners with all their guns!
Zadymilasja svecka vosku jarova,	A bright wax taper started smoking,
Podchodil molodoj puskar'	a young gunner
Ot k bocecke.	went up to the barrel.
A i s porochom-to bocka	And the barrel of gunpowder
Zakruzilasja.	started rolling.
Oj! Po podkopam pokatilasja,	Help! It rolled along the trenches
Da i chlopnula.	until it exploded.
Zavopili, zagaldeli zli tatarove,	The evil Tatars shrieked and

Blagim matom zalivlisja.	screamed, cursing in foul language.
Poleglo tatarovej t'ma t'muscaja,	Hordes of Tatars fell,
Poleglo ich sorok tysjacej datri tysjaci.	Forty-three thousand Tatars fell,
Tak-to, vo gorode bylo,	That's what happened
bo Kazani . . . É!	in Kazan . . . Hey!

ACT FOUR

Scene Two

Boris	**Boris**
Proscaj, moj syn, umiraju . . .	Farewell, my son, I am dying . . .
Sejcas ty carstvovat' nacnes'.	Now you will begin your reign.
Ne sprasivaj, kakim putem	Do not ask me by what means
Ja carstvo priobrel . . .	I obtained the crown . . .
Tebe ne nuzno znat'.	You need not to know.
Ty carstvovat' po pravu budes',	You will be a lawful ruler,
Kak moj naslednik,	as my successor,
Kak syn moj pervorodnyj . . .	as my firstborn son . . .
Syn moj! Ditja moe rodnoe!	My son! My dear child!
Ne vverjajsja navetam	Don't believe the slander
Bojar kramol'nych,	of the seditious boyars,
Zorko sledi za ich snosen'jami	keep a sharp watch on their secret
Tajnymi s Litvoju,	dealings with Lithuania.
Izmenu karaj bez poscady,	Punish treason harshly,
Bez milosti karaj;	punish without mercy;
Strogo vnikaj v sud narodnyj,	closely follow the judgment of
Sud nelicemernyj;	the people, they are impartial;
Stoj na straze borcom	defend and guard
Za veru pravuju,	the righteous faith,
Svjato cti svjatych ugodnikov	honour and respect the holy saints
boz' ich.	of the Lord.
Sestru tvoju, carevnu,	Look after your sister,
Sberegi, moj syn,	the Tsarevna, my son,
Ty ej odin chranitel' ostaes'sja . . .	you are now her only guardian . . .
Nasej Ksenii, golubke cistoj.	Our Xenia, the innocent dove
(almost spoken)	*(almost spoken)*

Gospodi! Gospodi!
Vozzri, molju,
Na slezy gresnogo otca;
Ne za sebja molju,
Ne za sebja, moj Boze!
S gornej nepristupnoj vysoty prolej
Ty blagodatnyj svet na cad moich,
Nevinnych . . . krotkich, cistych . . .

Sily nebesnye!
Strazi trona predvecnogo . . .
(he embraces his son)
Krylami svetlymi vy ochranite
Moe ditja rodnoe ot bed
i zol . . . ot iskusenij . . .
(He hugs his son and kisses him. Long-sustained chime of a bell and death knell.)

Boris

Zvon! Pogrebal'nyj zvon!

Pevcie (Monachi)

(offstage)
Plac'te, plac'te ljudie,
Nest' bo zizni v nem
I nemy usta ego
I ne dast otveta.
Plac'te. Alliluija!
(The boyars and the chorus come onto the stage.)

Boris

Nadgrobnyj vopl', schima . . .
Svjataja schima . . .
V monachi car' idet.

Feodor

Gosudar', uspokojsja!
Gospod' pomozet . . .

Oh Lord! Oh Lord!
Look down, I pray,
upon the tears of a sinful father;
I am not praying for myself,
not for myself, my Lord!
From your inaccessible height
pour down your blessed light
upon my children, my innocent . . .
sweet . . . pure children . . .
Oh, heavenly powers!
Guardians of the eternal throne . . .
(he embraces his son)
With your bright wings protect
my dear child from all evils and
calamity . . . from temptation . . .
(He hugs his son and kisses him. Long-sustained chime of a bell and death knell.)

Boris

A bell! A knell!

Chorus (Monks)

(offstage)
Weep, weep, oh people,
there is no life in him any more,
his lips are silent
and he will never give an answer.
Weep. Alleluia!
(The boyars and the chorus come onto the stage.)

Boris

Funeral wails, the monastic order . . .
The holy monastic order . . .
The Tsar is joining the monks.

Feodor

Your Majesty, calm down!
The Lord will help . . .

Boris

Net! Net, syn moj,
Cas moj probil . . .

Pevcie

Vizu mladenca umirajusca
I rydaju, placu,
Mjatetsja, trepescet on i k
pomosci vzyvaet
I net emu spasen'ja . . .
(they stop)

Boris

Boze! Boze! Tjazko mne!
Uze l' grecha
Ne zamolju!
O, zlaja smert'!
Kak mucis' ty zestoko!
(he jumps up)
Povremenite . . . ja car' esce!
*(he seizes his heart and falls into a
chair)*
Ja car' esce . . . Boze! Smert'!
(spoken)
Prosti menja!
(to the boyars, pointing to his son)
Vot, vot car' vas . . .
car' . . .
Prostite . . .
(in a whisper)
Prostite . . .

Bojare

(in a whisper)
Uspne!

Boris

No! No, my son,
my time has come . . .

Chorus

I can see the dying child,
and I weep and sob,
he tosses and turns and
calls for help,
but nothing can save him . . .
(they stop)

Boris

Oh Lord! Oh Lord! I feel terrible!
There is nothing I can do now
to atone for my sin!
Oh evil death!
How cruel are your torments!
(he jumps up)
Wait a minute . . . I am still Tsar!
*(he seizes his heart and falls into a
chair)*
I am still Tsar . . . Oh Lord! Death!
(spoken)
Forgive me!
(to the boyars, pointing to his son)
Here, here is your Tsar . . .
your Tsar . . .
Forgive me . . .
(in a whisper)
Forgive me . . .

Boyars

(in a whisper)
He has died!

———————□———————

Tosca
(1900)
Giacomo Puccini

Libretto by Giuseppe Giacosa and Luigi Illica

ACT TWO

In the Farnese Palace. Scarpia's room on the upper floor. The table is laid for supper. A large window gives onto the courtyard of the Palace. It is night.

Scarpia

(He is sitting at the table, having supper. From time to time he interrupts his meal to reflect. He takes a watch from his pocket, and in his restless demeanor he betrays a feverish anxiety.)

Tosca è un buon falco!
Certo a quest'ora
i miei segugi le
due prede azzannano!
Doman sul palco vedrà l'aurora
Angelotti e il bel Mario
al laccio pendere.
(He rings a handbell: Sciarrone appears.)
Tosca è a palazzo?

Sciarrone

Un ciambellan ne uscia pur
ora in traccia.

Scarpia

(pointing to the window)
Apri. Tarda è la notte.

(From the lower floor, where the Queen of Naples, Maria Carolina, is giving a great entertainment in honor of General Melas, is heard the sound of an orchestra.)

Alla cantata ancor manca
la Diva,
e strimpellan gavotte.

Scarpia

(He is sitting at the table, having supper. From time to time he interrupts his meal to reflect. He takes a watch from his pocket, and in his restless demeanor he betrays a feverish anxiety.)

Tosca is a good decoy!
By now my bloodhounds must
have sunk their teeth into their
two quarries!
Tomorrow's dawn will see
Angelotti and the handsome
Mario hanging on the gallows.
(He rings a handbell: Sciarrone appears.)
Is Tosca in the Palace?

Sciarrone

A footman has just gone to
fetch her.

Scarpia

(pointing to the window)
Open it. The hour is late.

The diva is not here yet for
the cantata,
and they're filling in with gavottes.

(to Sciarrone)
Tu attenderai la Tosca in
sull'entrata;
le dirai ch'io l'aspetto
finita la cantata . . .
o meglio . . .
(He rises and hurriedly writes a note.)
le darai questo biglietto.
*(Sciarrone goes out. Scarpia returns to
the table and pours himself a drink.)*
Ella verrà . . .
per amor del suo Mario!
Per amor del suo Mario
al piacer mio s'arrendarà.
Tal dei profondi amori è la
profonda miseria. Ha più forte
sapore la conquista violenta
che il mellifluo consenso.
Io di sospiri e di lattiginose
albe lunari poco m'appago.
Non so trarre accordi
di chitarra, né oròscopo di
fior, né far l'occhio di pesce,
o tubar come tortora!
Bramo. La cosa bramata
perseguo, me ne sazio e via la
getto volio a nuova
esca.
Dio creò diverse beltà,
vini diversi. Io vo' gustar
quanto più posso dell'opra divina!
(He drinks.)

(to Sciarrone)
You will wait for Tosca at
the entrance
and tell her that I expect her
when the cantata is over . . .
or still better . . .
(He rises and hurriedly writes a note.)
you will give her this note.
*(Sciarrone goes out. Scarpia returns to
the table and pours himself a drink.)*
She will come . . .
for love of her Mario!
For love of her Mario
she will submit to my pleasure.
The depth of her misery
will match the depth of her love.
A forcible conquest has a keener
relish than a willing surrender.
I find no delight in sighs and
sentimental moonlight serenades.
I cannot thrum chords on a
guitar, nor tell fortunes from
flower petals, nor make sheep's-
eyes or coo like a turtledove!
I have strong desires. I pursue
what I desire, glut myself with it
and discard it, turning to a new
diversion.
God created different beauties
and different wines. I wish to savor
all I can of what heaven produces!
(He drinks.)

©1997 The Teaching Company Limited Partnership

Scarpia

Ov'è Angelotti?

Cavaradossi

Non lo so.

Scarpia

Negate d'avergli date
cibo?

Cavaradossi

Nego!

Scarpia

E vesti?

Cavaradossi

Nego!

Scarpia

E asilo nella villa?
E che là sia nascosto?

Cavaradossi

Nego! nego!

Scarpia

Via, Cavaliere, riflettete:
saggia non è cotesta
ostinatezza vostra. Angoscia
grande, pronta confessione
evitarà! Io vi consiglio, dite:
dov'è dunque Angelotti?

Cavaradossi

Non lo so.

Scarpia

Ancor l'ultima volta.
Dov'è?

Scarpia

Where is Angelotti?

Cavaradossi

I don't know.

Scarpia

Do you deny having given him
food?

Cavaradossi

I do!

Scarpia

And clothes?

Cavaradossi

I deny it.

Scarpia

And sheltering him in your villa?
And that he is hidden there?

Cavaradossi

I deny everything.

Scarpia

Come, Cavaliere, reflect:
this obstinance of yours
is unwise. Prompt confession
could save you much anguish.
I advise you to tell me:
where is Angelotti?

Cavaradossi

I don't know.

Scarpia

Once more and for the last time:
where is he?

Cavaradossi

Non lo so!

Spoletta

(aside)
O bei tratti di corda!
(Enter Tosca, anxiously)

Scarpia

Eccola!

Tosca

(seeing Cavaradossi, runs to embrace him)
Mario, tu qui?!

Cavaradossi

(under his breath to Tosca, who gives a sign that she has understood)
Di quanto là vedesti, taci,
o m'uccidi!

Scarpia

Mario Cavaradossi, qual
testimone il Giudice v'aspetta.
(to Roberti)
Pria le forme ordinarie. Indi . . .
ai miei cenni.

Cavaradossi

I don't know!

Spoletta

(aside)
Now the cords will be tightened!
(Enter Tosca, anxiously)

Scarpia

Ah, there she is!

Tosca

(seeing Cavaradossi, runs to embrace him)
Mario, you here?

Cavaradossi

(under his breath to Tosca, who gives a sign that she has understood)
Say nothing of what you have seen
there, or it will mean my death!

Scarpia

Mario Cavaradossi, the judge
is waiting to take your deposition.
(to Roberti)
First the usual way. Afterwards...
as I indicate.

(The Judge goes into the torture chamber; the others follow, leaving Tosca and Scarpia alone. Spoletta withdraws to the door at the back of the room.)

Scarpia

Orsù, Tosca, parlate.

Tosca

Non so nulla!

Scarpia

Non vale quella prova?
Roberti, ripigliamo . . .

Tosca

No! Fermate! . . .

Scarpia

Voi parlerete?

Tosca

No . . . mostro!
lo strazi . . . l'uccidi!

Scarpia

Lo strazia quel vostro
silenzio assai più.

Scarpia

And now, Tosca, speak out.

Tosca

I know nothing!

Scarpia

That test was not enough?
Roberti, repeat the treatment . . .

Tosca

No! Stop!

Scarpia

Will you speak?

Tosca

No . . . you monster!
You are torturing him, killing him!

Scarpia

That silence of yours
is harming him far more.

Tosca

Tu ridi . . . tu ridi all'orrida
pena?

Scarpia

Mai Tosca alla scena più tragica
fu. Aprite le porte che
n'oda i lamenti.
*(Spoletta opens the door, placing
himself directly before it.)*

La voce di Cavaradossi

Vi sfido!

Scarpia

Più forte, più forte!

La voce di Cavaradossi

Vi sfido!

Scarpia

Parlate!

Tosca

Che dire?

Scarpia

Su, via!

Tosca

Ah! non so nulla!
Ah! dovrei mentir?

Scarpia

Dite dov'è Angelotti? Parlate, su,
via dove celato sta?

Tosca

Ah! più non posso! Ah!

Tosca

You laugh . . . at this terrible
suffering?

Scarpia

Tosca was never more tragic
on the stage! Open the doors so
that she can hear his cries!
*(Spoletta opens the door, placing
himself directly before it.)*

Cavaradossi's voice

I defy you!

Scarpia

Harder, harder!

Cavaradossi's voice

I defy you!

Scarpia

Speak!

Tosca

What can I say?

Scarpia

Come, quickly!

Tosca

Ah! I know nothing!
Must I tell lies?

Scarpia

Say where Angelotti is! Speak out
now! Where is he hidden?

Tosca

Ah! I cannot bear it!

cessate il martir! | Cease this torment!
È troppo soffrir! | It is too much to suffer!
Ah! non posso più! | Ah! I cannot bear it!

La voce di Cavaradossi

Ahimè!

Cavaradossi's voice

Ah!

(Tosca again turns imploringly to Scarpia, who signs to Spoletta to let her approach. She goes to the open door and, terrified at the sight of the dreadful scene, addresses Cavaradossi.)

Tosca

Mario, consenti ch'io parli? . . .

Tosca

Mario, will you let me speak?

La voce di Cavaradossi

No, no!

Cavaradossi's voice

No, no!

Tosca

Ascolta, non posso più . . .

Tosca

Listen: I can bear no more . . .

La voce di Cavaradossi

Stolta, che sai?
che puoi dir?

Cavaradossi's voice

Don't be silly! What do you know?
What can you say?

Scarpia

*(infuriated by Cavaradossi's words,
shouts at Spoletta)*
Ma fatelo tacere!

Scarpia

*(infuriated by Cavaradossi's words,
shouts at Spoletta)*
Make him be quiet!

(Spoletta enters the torture-chamber and comes out again shortly after, while Tosca, overcome by fearful agitation, falls prostrate on a settee and, her voice broken by sobs, appeals to Scarpia, who stands impassively in silence.)

Tosca

Che v'ho fatto in vita mia?
Son io
che così torturate! . . . Torturate
l'anima . . . Sì, mi torturate l'anima!

Tosca

What harm have I ever done you?
It is I whom you are torturing so!
You are torturing my soul . . .
Yes, it is my soul you are torturing!

Spoletta

(muttering a prayer)
Judex ergo cum sedebit
Quidquid latet apparebit,
Nil inultum remanebit.

(Scarpia, profiting by Tosca's prostration, goes to the torture-chamber and signals for the torture to recommence.)

La voce di Cavaradossi

Ah!

Tosca

(At Cavaradossi's cry she leaps up and in a stifled voice hurriedly says to Scarpia:)
Nel pozzo . . . nel giardino . . .

Scarpia

Là è l'Angelotti?

Tosca

Sì . . .

Scarpia

Basta, Roberti.

Sciarrone

(appearing at the door)
È svenuto!

Tosca

(to Scarpia)
Assassino! . . . Voglio vederlo . . .

Scarpia

Portatelo qui.

Spoletta

(muttering a prayer)
Judex ergo cum sedebit
Quidquid latet apparebit,
Nil inultum remanebit.

Cavaradossi's voice

Ah!

Tosca

(At Cavaradossi's cry she leaps up and in a stifled voice hurriedly says to Scarpia)
In the well . . . in the garden . . .

Scarpia

Angelotti is there?

Tosca

Yes . . .

Scarpia

That will do, Roberti.

Sciarrone

(appearing at the door)
He has fainted!

Tosca

(to Scarpia)
Murderer! . . . I want to see him ...

Scarpia

Carry him in.

———————□———————

(Cavaradossi, who has been listening with growing anxiety to Sciarrone's words, in his enthusiasm finds the strength to rise and confront Scarpia menacingly.)

Cavaradossi

Vittoria! Vittoria!
L'alba vindice appar
che fa gli empi tremar!
Libertà sorge, crollan
tirannidi!

Tosca

(in despair, holding Cavaradossi close, trying to calm him)
Mario, taci, pietà di me!

Cavaradossi

Del sofferto martir
me vedrai qui gioir . . .
il tuo cuor trema, o Scarpia,
carnefice!

Scarpia

Braveggia, urla! T'affretta
a palesarmi il fondo
dell'alma ria!
Va! Moribondo,
il capestro t'aspetta!
(shouts to the police)
Portatemelo via!

Cavaradossi

Victory! Victory
Let the dawn of vengeance appear
to strike terror into our foes!
Let freedom arise
and tyrants be overthrown!

Tosca

(in despair, holding Cavaradossi close, trying to calm him)
Hush, Mario, for my sake!

Cavaradossi

You shall see me rejoice
for the anguish I have suffered . . .
Let your heart falter,
O Scarpia, you butcher!

Scarpia

Bluster and bawl!
Hasten to reveal to me
the depths of your infamous soul!
Go! The gallows awaits you,
half dead as you already are.
(shouts to the police)
Take him out of here!

(Sciarrone and the police-agents seize Cavaradossi and drag him towards the door. Tosca tries to oppose them with all her strength, clinging to Mario.)

Tosca

Ah . . . Mario, Mario . . .
con te . . .

Scarpia

(pushing her back and closing the door)
Voi no!

Tosca

Ah . . . Mario, Mario . . .
I will go with you . . .

Scarpia

(pushing her back and closing the door)
Not you!

Tosca

*(sits facing Scarpia, looking him
straight in the eye)*
Quanto?

Scarpia

Quanto?

Tosca

Il prezzo!

Scarpia

Già. Mi dicon venal,
ma a donna bella non mi vendo
a prezzo di moneta.
Se la giurata fede devo
tradir, ne voglio
altra mercede.
Quest'ora io l'attendeva.
Già mi struggea
l'amor della diva! . . .
Ma poc'anzi ti mirai
qual non ti vidi mai!
Quel tuo pianto era lava ai sensi
miei e il tuo sguardo
che odio in me dardeggiava,
mie brame inferociva!
Agil qual leopardo t'avvinghiasti
all'amante, ah, in quell'istante
t'ho giurata mia!

Tosca

*(sits facing Scarpia, looking him
straight in the eye)*
How much?

Scarpia

How much?

Tosca

What's your price?

Scarpia

Ah! They call me venal,
but I don't sell myself
to lovely ladies for mere money.
If I have to betray my sworn
loyalty, I choose
a different payment.
I've been waiting for this moment.
Love of the diva
has long consumed me! . . .
But a while ago I saw you
as I had never seen you before!
Your tears flowed like lava
on my senses, and your eyes,
which darted hatred at me,
made my desire all the fiercer!
When, supple as a leopard, you
clung to your lover, ah, in that moment I swore you should be mine!

*(He advances upon Tosca with open arms; she, who had been listening motion-
less, petrified, to his lascivious words, suddenly rises and takes refuge behind the
settee.)*

Tosca

Ah!

Tosca

Ah!

"Vissi d'Arte"

Tosca

(Overcome by grief, she falls onto the settee. Scarpia coldly continues to gaze at her.)
Vissi d'arte,
vissi d'amore,
non feci mai male ad anima viva!
Con man furtiva quante
miserie conobbi, aiutai.
Sempre con fe' sincera
la mia preghiera
ai santi tabernacoli sali,
sempre con fe' sincera
diedi fiori agli altar.
Nell'ora del dolore
perché, perché, Signore,
perché me ne rimuneri così?
Diedi gioielli della Madonna
al manto, e diedi il canto agli
astri, al ciel, che ne ridean
più belli.
Nell'ora del dolor
perché, perché, Signore,
perché me ne rimuneri così?

Tosca

(Overcome by grief, she falls onto the settee. Scarpia coldly continues to gaze at her.)
I have lived for art,
I have lived for love,
and never harmed a living soul!
In secret I have given aid to as
many unfortunates as I have
known. Always a true believer,
I have offered up my prayers
at the holy shrines;
always a true believer,
I have laid flowers on the altar.
In my hour of tribulation
why, O Lord, why
hast Thou repaid me thus?
I gave jewels for the Madonna's
mantle, and offered my singing
to the starry heavens, that they
might smile more brightly.
In my hour of tribulation
why, O Lord, why
hast Thou repaid me thus?

———□———

Scarpia

Io tenni la promessa . . .

Scarpia

I have kept my promise . . .

Tosca

Non ancora.
Voglio un salvacondotto, onde
fuggir dallo Stato con lui.

Tosca

Not yet.
I want a safe-conduct so
that I can flee the State with him.

Scarpia

Partir dunque volete?

Scarpia

Then you want to leave?

Tosca

Sì, per sempre!

Scarpia

Si adempia il voler vostro.
(*He goes to a desk and begins to write,
breaking off to ask Tosca*)
E qual via scegliete?

Tosca

La più breve!

Scarpia

Civitavecchia?

Tosca

Sì.

Tosca

Yes, for good!

Scarpia

You shall have your way.
(*He goes to a desk and begins to write,
breaking off to ask Tosca*)
Which road will you take?

Tosca

The shortest!

Scarpia

Civitavecchia?

Tosca

Yes.

(*While Scarpia is writing, Tosca approaches the table and with a trembling hand
takes the glass of Spanish wine poured out by Scarpia; but as she raises it to her
lips she perceives on the table a sharp-pointed knife. She casts a rapid glance at
Scarpia who at that moment is busy writing, and with infinite caution succeeds
in taking possession of the knife. She hides it behind her, leaning on the table and
watching Scarpia. Having finished writing the safe-conduct and put his seal to it,
he folds the paper; then opening his arms, he advances on Tosca to embrace her.*)

Scarpia

Tosca, finalmenti mia! . . .
(*But his tone of rapture changes to a
terrible cry; Tosca has stabbed him to
the heart.*)
Maledetta!!!

Tosca

Questo è il bacio di Tosca!
(*Scarpia, staggering, tries to clutch at
Tosca, who recoils in terror.*)

Scarpia

Aiuto . . . muoio . . .

Scarpia

Tosca, at last you are mine!
(*But his tone of rapture changes to a
terrible cry; Tosca has stabbed him to
the heart.*)
A curse on you!

Tosca

That was Tosca's kiss!
(*Scarpia, staggering, tries to clutch at
Tosca, who recoils in terror.*)

Scarpia

Help! . . . I'm dying! . . .

soccorso . . . muoio . . .	Help! . . . I'm dying! . . .

Tosca	**Tosca**
It soffoca il sangue? Ah!	Is your blood choking you? Ah!
E ucciso da una donna . . .	Slain by a woman! . . .
M'hai assai	You tortured me so!
torturata! Odi to ancora? Parla!	Can you still hear?
Guardami!	Speak! Look at me!
Son Tosca, o Scarpia!	This is Tosca, O Scarpia!

Scarpia	**Scarpia**
Soccorso! . . . aiuto!	Help! . . . Help!

Tosca	**Tosca**
Ti soffoca il	Are you choking in your own
sangue? . . .	blood? . . .
Muori, dannato! muori!! muori!!!	Die you fiend! Die! Die!!
È morto . . .	He is dead! . . .
Or gli perdono! . . .	Now I forgive him . . .

(Without taking her eyes off Scarpia's body, she goes to the table, takes a bottle of water and, dipping a napkin in it, washes her fingers: then she rearranges her hair in front of the mirror. Remembering the safe-conduct, she looks for it on the desk but cannot find it: she searches elsewhere and finally sees it clutched in Scarpia's stiffening hand. She lifts his arm, then lets it fall inert after having taken the safe-conduct, which she hides in her bosom.)

E avanti a lui tremava tutta Roma!	And all Rome used to tremble before him!

(On the point of leaving, she changes her mind; she goes and takes the two candles from the wall-bracket on the left and lights them from the candlesticks on the table, which she then extinguishes. She places one candle to the right of Scarpia's head, the other to the left. She looks round again and, seeing a crucifix, takes it from the wall and, carrying it reverently, kneels down and places it on Scarpia's breast. She rises and very cautiously goes out, closing the door behind her.)

Capriccio
(1941)
Richard Strauss
Libretto by Clemens Krauss and the composer

Olivier

Tanz und Musik stehen im Bann des Rhythmus, ihm unterworfen seit ewiger Zeit.

Flamand

Deiner Verse Mass ist ein weit stärkerer Zwang.

Olivier

Frei schaltet in ihm des Dichters Gedanke! Wer zieht da die Grenze zwischen Form und Gehalt?

Flamand

In irdischer Form ein Unfaßbar-Höheres: Musik! Sie erhebt sich in Sphären, in die der Gedanke nicht dringt.

Olivier

Nicht in unfassbaren Klängen, in klarer Sprache forme ich meine Gedanken. Dies ist der Musik für immer verwehrt.

Flamand

Mein Gedanke is die Melodie. Sie kündet Tieferes, ein Unaussprechliches! In einem Akkord erlebst du eine Welt.

Direktor

Sie streiten um eine Rangordnung

Olivier (Poet)

Music and dance are the slaves of rhythm, they have served it since the beginning of time.

Flamand (Composer)

There is more constraint in the restrictions of verse.

Olivier

Freedom of ideas is given to poets. Who sees any boundary between content and form?

Flamand

Music is in every respect more full of meaning, it ascends in spheres which you cannot invade with the mind.

Olivier

Not in musical abstraction but in the clearest language can I express what I'm thinking. This is what your music can never achieve.

Flamand

My ideas exist as melodies, and what they mean to me is inexpressible. In one single chord you feel all the world.

La Roche (Director)

They are fighting; each one claims

ihrer Künste. Verlorene Mühe! Im Bereich meiner Bühne dienen sie alle.

Graf

Schon sind wir inmitten der Diskussion über das Streit-Thema unserer Tage.

Flamand

Musik is eine erhabene Kunst! Nur unwilling dient sie dem Trug des Theaters.

Gräfin

Nicht Trug! Die Bühne enthüllt uns das Geheimnis der Wirklichkeit. Wie in einem Zauberspiegel gewahren wir uns selbst. Das Theater ist das ergreifende Sinnbild des Lebens.

Direktor

Seine oberste Göttin: Phantasie. Ihr untertan alle Künste: Poesie, Malerei, Skulptur und Musik. Und wo wär' eure Sprache, was sind eure Töne ohne Deklamation und Gesang? Ohne die Darstellung durch den Akteur, den Zauber seiner Persönlichkeit, ohne sein Kostüm? He? Ohne seine Maske?

Clairon

Jawohl, ganz recht!

Direktor

Ihr überschätzt euren Schreibtisch!

---

more importance for his art. I could spare them the trouble! In the realm of my stage they are nothing but servants.

Count

Again we arrive at the argument, always a topic for wide discussion.

Flamand

I find in music exalted art, reluctant to serve the domain of the theatre.

Countess

My friend! The theatre unveils for us the secrets of reality. Ever in its magic mirror we discover ourselves. The theatre moves us because it is reality's symbol.

La Roche

It is ruled by the goddess of invention. All the arts are her servants: be it poetry, be it painting, sculpture or music. What would become of your language, and what of your music if no actors were there to perform? Lacking the art of the actor, his magic personality, lacking all these where would you be? Eh? Or without his costume?

Clairon (Actress)

Indeed!

La Roche

You overvalue your labors.

Olivier

Der dichtende Geist ist der Spiegel
der Welt. Poesie ist die Mutter aller
Künste!

Flamand

Musik ist die Wurzel, der alles
entquillt. Die Klänge der Natur
singen das Wiegenlied allen Künsten!

Olivier

Die sprache des Menschen allein ist
der Boden, dem sie entspriessen.

Flamand

Der Schmerzensschrei ging der
Sprache voraus!

Olivier

Doch das Leid zu deuten vermag sie
allein. Der wirklichen Tiefe des
Tragischen kann nur die Dichtkunst
Ausdruck verleihen. Nie kann sie sich
in Tönen offenbaren!

Gräfin

Das sagt Ihr jetzt, in dem Augenblick,
wo ein Genie uns lehrt, daß es eine
musikalische Tragödie gibt?

Graf

Halt! Noch einen Schritt und wir
stehen vor dem Abgrund! Schon
stehen wir der "Oper" Aug in Aug
gegenüber.

Gräfin

Ein schöner Anblick,
ich wag' es zu sagen.

Olivier

The poet's idea is the mirror of life.
All the arts must call poetry their
mother!

Flamand

But music is the root from which
everything springs. And Nature's
voices sing all other arts to sleep in
their cradles.

Olivier

The language of mankind alone is
the soil where art can be nourished.

Flamand

The cry of pain preceded all speech!

Olivier

But in language only can pain be
defined. Tragedy finds its expression
only when a poet puts it into words.
Music has not the power to reveal it.

Countess

How can you say such a thing today
just when a genius proves it is
possible to write a musical tragedy?

Count

Stop! One more step and we stand
before the abyss. I fear that we are
standing face to face with an opera.

Countess

A charming vision,
I venture to say.

Clairon

Etwas absonderlich, dieses Geschöpf aus Tönen und Worten.

Graf

(interrupting her)
Und Rezitativen! Und Rezitativen!

Olivier

Komponist und Dichter, einer vom andern schrecklich behindert verschwenden unsägliche Mühen, um es zur Welt zu bringen.

Graf

Eine Oper is ein absurdes Ding. Befehle werden singend erteilt, über Politik im Duett verhandelt. Man tanzt um ein Grab, und Dolchstiche werden melodisch verabreicht.

Clairon

Somewhat peculiar, this combination of music and language.

Count

(interrupting her)
And recitatives! And recitatives!

Olivier

The composer and poet, dreadfully hampered each by the other, are wasting unspeakable labor in giving birth to opera and acting as its midwives.

Count

Every opera is in itself absurd: a murder plot is hatched in a song; all affairs of state are discussed in chorus; they dance round a grave and suicide takes place to music.

———◻———

How to Listen to and Understand Opera
Timeline

c. 1440..............................Josquin des Prez born (d. 1521)

c. 1546..............................Giulio Caccini born (d. 1618)

1561 ....Jacopo Peri born (d. c.1633)

1562 ....Ottavio Rinuccini born (d.1621)

1567 ....Claudio Monteverdi born (d. 1643)

1573–1592.........................Florentine Camerata

1588 ....English defeat Spanish Armada

1598 ....*Daphne*, considered first opera, by Peri and Corsi

1600 ....Peri's *Euridice*

1604 ....Shakespeare's *Othello*

1607 ....Monteverdi's *Orfeo*

1618 ....Beginning of Thirty Years' War

1630 ....Boston founded by Puritans

1632 ....Jean-Baptiste Lully born (d. 1687)

1649 ....King Charles I of England beheaded

1660 ....Alessandro Scarlatti born (d. 1725)

1661 ....Louis XIV becomes King of France

1675 ....Antonio Vivaldi born (d. 1741)

1683 ....Jean-Philippe Rameau born (d. 1764)

1685 ....Revocation of Edict of Nantes in France

1687 ....Isaac Newton's *Principia Mathematica*

1688 ....England's Glorious Revolution

1698 ....Pietro Metastasio born (d. 1782)

1712 ....Jean-Jacques Rousseau born (d. 1778)

1710 ....Giovanni Battista Pergolesi born (d. 1736)

1714 ....Christoph Willibald von Gluck born (d. 1787)

1715 ....Scarlatti's *Tigrane*

1719 ....Rediscovery of Pompeii

1733 ....Pergolesi's *La serva padrona*

1751 ....First volumes of French Encyclopedia

1756 ....Wolfgang Amadeus Mozart born (d.1791)

1776 ....Declaration of Independence

1781 ....Mozart's *Idomeneo*

1786 ....Mozart's *Marriage of Figaro*

1786 ....Carl Maria von Weber born (d. 1826)

1788 ....Arthur Schopenhauer born (d. 1860)

1789 ....French Revolution begins

1791 ....Mozart's *The Magic Flute*

1791 ....Giacomo Meyerbeer born (d. 1864)

1792 ....Gioacchino Antonio Rossini born (d. 1868)

1797 ....Gaetano Donizetti born (d. 1848)

1801 ....Vincenzo Bellini born (d. 1835)

1804 ....Mikhail Glinka born (d. 1857)

1808 ....Goethe's *Faust*

1813 ....Giuseppe Verdi born (d. 1901)

1813 ....Richard Wagner born (d. 1883)

1815	Battle of Waterloo
1833	Aleksandr Borodin born (d. 1887)
1835	Cesar Cui born (d. 1918)
1837	Mili Balakirev born (d. 1910)
1838	Queen Victoria crowned
1838	George Bizet born (d. 1875)
1839	Modest Mussorgsky born (d. 1881)
1841	Saxophone invented
1842	Glinka's *Russlan and Lyudmila*
1844	Nicolai Rimsky-Korsakov born (d. 1908)
1848	*Communist Manifesto* by Marx and Engels
1853	Crimean War begins
1858	Giacomo Puccini born (d. 1924)
1859	Wagner's *Tristan und Isolde*
1861	Russian serfs emancipated
1863	Lincoln's Gettysburg Address
1864	Richard Strauss born (d.1949)
1868–69	Mussorgsky's *Boris Godunov*
1869	Opening of Suez Canal
1870	Franco-Prussian War
1877	Invention of phonograph
1900	Freud's *The Interpretation of Dreams*
1900	Puccini's *Tosca*
1901	Boer War
1905	Einstein's Special Theory of Relativity

1918 ....Armistice ending First World War
1920 ....League of Nations formed
1939 ....Beginning of World War II
1941 ....Strauss's *Capriccio*

Glossary

Aria: The general term for an extended solo in opera—the equivalent of a soliloquy—which brings the action and "real time" to a temporary halt, and in which the character expresses his or her feelings about the action and events just described. Arias generally have a high melodic profile and are typically accompanied by the full orchestra.

Aria da capo: A baroque aria form schematized as A-B-A′. An initial musical phrase (A) is followed by a contrasting passage (B). The initial phrase is then recapitulated but now embellished and ornamented by the singer.

Arioso: A sung passage with enough melodic contour to sound aria-like, but which has a syllabic sort of setting and the narrative quality of a recitative.

Baritone: The middle category of male voice, higher in range and lighter in timbre than bass, but lower and heavier than tenor.

Bass: The lowest category male voice—rich, dark, heavy, and powerful.

Basso profundo: An unusually deep bass voice.

Bel canto opera: A style of early-19th-century Italian opera that stresses simple, songlike melodies and harmonic accompaniment and that cultivates a highly decorous style of singing.

Cadenza: A florid, improvised passage to be performed by singers before the final bars of an aria or movement.

Castrato: A male soprano whose soprano voice has been preserved by castration prior to puberty.

Cavatina: A slow and lyric aria meant to display the singer's breath control, line, and beauty of tone.

Coloratura: Literally, "coloration" or "coloring." As used in music, the term refers to brilliantly ornamented writing for the voice, or to the type of voice agile enough to specialize in such music.

Coloratura soprano: The highest of the soprano voices, characterized by broad range, clear quality, and exceptional agility.

Comic opera: An expression sometimes used in English either as a translation of the French opéra comique or the Italian opera buffa.

Commedia dell'arte: Traveling musical companies that originated in 16th-century Italy. Their performances led eventually to comic opera.

Contralto: The lowest category of female voice.

Countertenor: An exceptionally high male voice, comparable to the female contralto.

Dramatic voice: A heavier, darker, and more forceful voice than a lyric voice; used in reference to soprano, tenor, and baritone voices.

Ensemble: Continuously sung passages in which any number of singers may participate. Ensembles were typically used to end acts. They reached their highest state of development in opera buffa.

***Gesamtkunstwerk*:** "The all-inclusive art form," Richard Wagner's term for his all-encompassing music dramas.

Grand opera: A spectacular and dramatic genre of opera, developed in early-19th-century France and designed to appeal especially to the middle class. This term is often used to refer to 19th-century opera in general.

Homophony: A melodic texture in which one melody line predominates with all other musical material heard as secondary or as accompaniment.

Intermezzo: A comic interlude inserted between the acts of Italian opera seria during the second half of the 17th century and the first half of the 18th century.

Intermezzo/Intermedio: Musical prologues and interludes inserted into the spoken Italian dramas of the late 16th century.

Leitmotif: A theme or motive associated with a particular person, thing, or dramatic idea.

Libretto: Literally "little book." The verbal text of an opera, written for the composer to set to music.

Lyric opera: An operatic genre that combines opéra comique's use of spoken dialogue and direct, appealing melodies with grand opera's tendency toward numerous performers and grandiose singing.

Lyric voice: A fairly light, warm, clear, and flexible voice; used in reference to soprano, tenor, and baritone voices.

Madrigal: A work for four to six voices that freely mixes polyphonic and homophonic textures and uses word-painting.

Melodrama: A genre of musical theater that combines spoken dialogue with background music.

Mezzo-soprano: The middle category of female voice, between contralto and soprano.

Monophony: A melodic texture consisting of a single unaccompanied melody line.

Music drama: An operatic form created by Richard Wagner. Refers to a through-composed operatic work which stresses dramatic and psychological content and in which voices and orchestra are completely intertwined and of equal importance.

Opera: A drama which combines soliloquy, dialogue, scenery, action, and continuous (or nearly continuous) music, the whole greater than the parts.

Opera buffa: A general designation for Italian operas of the middle and late 18th century that do not come under the heading of opera seria. These productions were melodically simpler and more "popular" than Baroque opera seria.

Opéra comique: A popular French operatic genre that developed concurrently with grand opera in the early 19th century but employed spoken dialogue rather than recitative and featured somewhat less pretentious productions than grand opera.

Opera seria: "Serious" opera of the Baroque era—elaborate and grandiose productions typically based on subjects from ancient history and/or mythology.

Operetta: Literally, "little opera." During the 19th century, the term came to mean a lighter type of opera, usually with spoken dialogue separating the musical numbers.

Overture: An instrumental prelude to an opera.

Parlante: Literally, "talking"; a compositional technique used by Giuseppe Verdi and other late-19th-century operatic composers in which recitative-like vocal lines were underlaid with continuous thematic music played by the orchestra.

Pastoral: The style of dramatic poetry that dominated Italian theater in the late 16th and early 17th centuries, featuring sylvan settings and mild love adventures and usually ending happily.

Polyphony: A melodic texture consisting of two or more simultaneous melody lines of equal importance.

Recitative: A style of writing for the voice in which the rhythms and inflections of speech are retained. In opera, it is used for action, dialogue, and narrative. Recitatives are most typically *secco* or "dry" (i.e., accompanied only by *basso continuo*).

Ritornello: An instrumental refrain.

Sinfonia: An independent musical piece that acts as an introduction or a postlude.

Singspiel: German for "sing-play." Refers to a partly sung, partly spoken German theatrical genre with its roots in popular culture.

Soprano: The highest category of female voice.

Spinto soprano: The soprano voice lying between the lyric and dramatic soprano voices and having qualities of both.

Tenor: The highest category of male voice.

Tone poem: A purely instrumental work that tells a specific story and invokes explicit imagery; a term created by Richard Strauss.

Verismo opera: A genre of opera characterized by dramatic and expressive realism and naturalism, especially in the portrayal of people, events, and emotions. This genre was popular among Italian and French opera composers in the late 19th and early 20th centuries.

Voci bianchi: Literally, "white voices," referring to those of the *castrati*.

Word-painting: A compositional technique that seeks to form an expressive syntax by matching literary descriptions with corresponding musical events; this technique is characteristic of madrigals.

Biographical Notes

Bernard de Ventadorn (circa 1150–'80). Important French troubadour poet and composer of the second half of the 12th century.

Bizet, Georges (1838–'75). French opera composer famous for *Carmen*, his greatest work and the most popular opera of all time. A master dramatist, Bizet deftly establishes character and mood through his music.

Boito, Arrigo (1842–1918). Italian librettist and composer. Boito's libretti for Verdi's *Otello* and *Falstaff* are considered among the greatest in all Italian opera.

Da Ponte, Lorenzo (1749–1838). Italian librettist and poet. Da Ponte rose to the peak of his achievement with his libretti for Mozart's operas *The Marriage of Figaro*, *Don Giovanni* and *Così fan tutte*.

Caccini, Giulio (1551–1618). One of the earliest Italian opera composers and a member of the Florentine Camerata.

Gesualdo, Carlo, Prince of Venosa (circa 1560–1613). Italian lutenist and composer, famous for his innovations of harmonic progressions and dissonance.

Glinka, Mikhail (1804–'57). Russian composer regarded as the founder of Russian musical nationalism. His operatic masterpiece is *Ruslan and Lyudmila* of 1836.

Gluck, Christoph Willibald (1714–'87). Major composer who effected a synthesis of elements of Italian opera and traditional French opera. Essential features of his operatic style include melodically simple and emotionally direct arias; recitatives that demonstrate a high melodic content; the use of dance as integral to the dramatic action; strong reliance on choruses, and a high degree of integration of dance, chorus and solos.

Hofmannsthal, Hugo von (1874–1929). Great Austrian librettist who wrote the libretti for many of Richard Strauss's operas.

Josquin des Prez (circa 1440–1521). Preeminent composer of the Renaissance who used both polyphonic and homophonic styles. His madrigals represent the Renaissance ideal of emotional and character expressivity.

Leonin (Magister Leoninus) (circa 1135–circa 1201). Composer and poet of the Notre Dame school and greatest exponent of florid organum.

Lully, Jean-Baptiste (1632–'87). Major French composer, who laid the foundation for the French operatic tradition. Lully created a national style that focused on magnificence, tragic drama and dance. He designed a type of recitative that was modeled on spoken drama, using one pitch per syllable and reflecting the flexibility of the French language, with its continuous changes of meter. His arias tend to be short and limited in vocal range, with an emphasis on clear enunciation.

Machaut, Guillaume de (circa 1300–'77). Important composer of sacred and secular music; master of polyphonic technique and musical eloquence.

Mahler, Gustav (1860–1911). Great Austrian composer and opera conductor of the late romantic era. Although he never wrote an opera, Mahler was a master of smaller-scale vocal music and his orchestral music has deep affinities with vocal music in its expressive content.

Metastasio, Pietro (1698–1782). Greatest librettist of the first half of the 18th century. Metastasio standardized his libretti into a formulaic dramatic procedure and formularized arias into a structure known as the "da capo" aria. His reforms influenced the development of opera seria.

Meyerbeer, Giacomo (1791–1864). German-born composer who almost single-handedly established French grand opera. Meyerbeer was famous for his ability to manage enormous forces on stage. His most famous opera is *Les Huguenots* of 1836. His operas have fallen into obscurity because they lack musical and dramatic substance.

Monteverdi, Claudio (1567–1643). Italian composer credited with the creation of the first opera, *Orfeo* of 1607. Monteverdi did not invent opera, but elevated it to a level of artistic viability and substance it had not previously enjoyed. His most important contribution to the genre was an elevated form of recitative: *arioso*. He was the first composer to use purely instrumental passages in ensemble numbers in opera. He was in advance of his time in his use of dissonance and chromatic harmonies and in his ability to express fundamental emotions through music. Many of his operas are still performed today.

Mozart, Wolfgang Amadeus (1756–'91). Great Austrian composer of the classical era. His operas are widely regarded as his greatest contribution to musical history. A major aspect of Mozart's significance as an opera composer is his unprecedented genius for musical characterization and dramatic momentum. He is a consummate master of complex and subtle vocal and orchestral manipulation. Mozart's music does not just decorate the libretto. It creates a whole new drama, revealing subtleties and truths that go beyond the libretto. It energizes the dramatic action and fleshes out his characters, imbuing them with an extraordinary range of moods, emotions, subtlety, unconscious motivation and humanity.

Mussorgsky, Modest (1839–'81). Great Russian composer and member of the so-called Russian Five, a group of composers who established the Russian national style of the mid to late 19th century. His opera *Boris Godunov* is the pinnacle of Russian opera.

Pergolesi, Giovanni (1710–'36). Italian composer of *La serva padrona* (1733), the first important opera buffa that laid the foundation for subsequent contributions to the genre.

Peri, Jacopo (1561–1633). One of the earliest Italian opera composers and member of the Florentine Camerata. Peri is known for his operas *Daphne* and *Euridice*.

Puccini, Giacomo (1858–1924). Great Italian composer of universally popular operas. Puccini was the greatest exponent of the opera verismo style, which found inspiration in the dark side of human nature. He was a superb lyricist and consummate dramatist. Among his best-loved and renowned operas are *Madam Butterfly, Tosca* and *La Bohème*.

Rameau, Jean-Philippe (1683–1764). Foremost French composer of the 18th century. Rameau's operas display much less contrast between aria and recitative than contemporary Italian operas. Although Rameau's operas are rarely heard outside France because they are tailored to particular French tastes, they are worth seeking out for their musical value.

Rinuccini, Ottavio (1562–1621). Italian poet/librettist and member of the Florentine Camerata. Rinuccini wrote the libretti for the earliest operas: Caccini's *Euridice* and Peri's *Daphne*.

Rossini, Gioacchino (1792–1868). Greatest Italian composer of the bel canto style. Rossini had a great gift for wit, comedy and compositional innovation. He pioneered the use of strings instead of harpsichord or piano to accompany recitative. He invented the long, orchestral type of crescendo known as the "Rossini crescendo." He was a master of orchestral color and musical characterization. His opera, *The Barber of Seville* remains one of the best-loved and greatest comic operas of all time. Its most famous aria, "Largo al factotum," introduces the character of Figaro and is a brilliant example of musical characterization.

Rousseau, Jean-Jacques (1712–'78). Swiss-born French philosopher and composer who embraced the Italian opera buffa genre as an example of opera appropriate to the Enlightenment. His *Le Devin du village* (1752) is very close to the popular French tradition of opéra comique.

Scarlatti, Alessandro (1660–1725). Founder of the Neapolitan school of opera, Scarlatti's operas exerted substantial influence on other opera composers.

Strauss, Richard (1864–1949). Brilliant German composer, whose music stretches Wagnerian concepts to further limits. Strauss's psychopathological and erotic masterpiece *Salome* represents experimental, post-Victorian trends at the turn of the 20th century.

Verdi, Giuseppe (1813–1901). Greatest Italian opera composer of the second half of the 19th century. Verdi's operas endure because of their use of well-written libretti, their melodic beauty, their focus on human emotions, their psychological insight, and their unsurpassed dramatic power. Among Verdi's greatest operas are *Rigoletto*, *La Traviata* and *Otello*.

Wagner, Richard (1813–'83). Great German composer whose operas revolutionized music and whose opera, *Tristan und Isolde* is considered, along with Beethoven's Ninth Symphony, the most influential composition of the 19th century. Wagner developed the concept of the music drama (*Gesamtkunstwerk*) as an artistic genre that encompasses all types of art: drama, music, poetry, dance, etc. He created the leitmotif whereby musical motives are assigned to characters, things or concepts and he gave the orchestra unprecedented power as the purveyor of inner meanings and unspoken truths.

Weber, Carl Maria von (1786–1826). German composer whose opera *Der Freischütz* became the definitive work that established 19th-century German opera, characterized by the use of spoken dialogue, and plots that hinge on the supernatural as found in German medieval legend.

Weelkes, Thomas (circa 1575–1623). One of the great English madrigal composers. Weelkes was a master of word painting.

How to Listen to and Understand Opera
Selective Bibliography

General Sources

Donington, Robert. *Opera and its Symbols*. Yale University Press, 1990.

Grout, Donald. *A Short History of Opera*. 2d ed. Columbia University Press, 1965.

Grout, Donald, and Claude Palisca. *A History of Western Music*. 5th ed. W.W. Norton, 1996.

Hamm, Charles. *Opera*. Allyn and Bacon, 1966.

Kerman, Joseph. *Opera as Drama*. University of California Press, 1988.

Mordden, Ethan. *Opera Anecdotes*. 1985. Reprint, Norton, 1996.

New Grove Dictionary of Music, The. Macmillan Publishers, 1980.

Palisca, Claude, ed. *Norton Anthology of Western Music*. 3d ed. W.W. Norton, 1980.

Plaut, Eric. *Grand Opera—Mirror of the Western Mind*. Ivan R. Dcc, 1993.

Schonberg, Harold. *The Lives of the Great Composers*. Norton, 1970.

Weiss, Piero, and Richard Taruskin. *Music in the Western World*. Schirmer, 1984.

Italian Opera

Kimbell, David. *Italian Opera*. Cambridge University Press, 1991.

Mozart

Dent, Edward. *Mozart's Operas*. Clarendon/Oxford University Press, 1991.

Heartz, Daniel. *Mozart's Operas*. University of California Press, 1990.

Mann, William. *The Operas of Mozart*. Oxford University Press, 1977.

Puccini

Osborne, Charles. *The Complete Operas of Puccini*. Atheneum, 1982.

Strauss

Del Mar, Normen. *Richard Strauss—A Critical Commentary of His Life and Works*. Cornell University Press, 1986.

Verdi

Hepokoski, James. *Otello*. Cambridge University Press, 1987.
Budden, Julien. *The Operas of Verdi*. Cassell, 1973.
Phillips-Matz. *Verdi*. Oxford University Press, 1993.

Wagner

Magee, Brian. *Aspects of Wagner*. Oxford University Press, 1988.
Millington, Barry. *Wagner*. Princeton University Press, 1984.